**Al**

# Always Three—A Trilogy

THREE SHORT STORIES OF BIBLICAL ADVICE AND ADMONITIONS

CHERYL MAJOR BRANDON, EdD

This book was printed in the United Slates of America.



To order additional copies of this book, contact:
cheryljuly1@yahoo.com

# Table of Contents

## Foreword by Dr. Gwendolyn King Honorè

"This thought-provoking book includes three works, One of which is, "Lilith the First Wife." This work brings various biblical actions to life and make Scriptures comprehensible in a highly creative way. The writer takes the reader on a journey, detailing how the enemy attacks the mind and how simplistic behavior can alter a person's obedience to God. My mind was enlightened even more to the deceitfulness of the enemy, in his efforts to pull in those who have not fully committed themselves to God."

Dr. Gwendolyn King (Perry) Honorè holds a Doctor of Ministry in Theology and Counseling from Life Christian University and is author of *Wise Wives Don't Run but Sometime They Wanna!'* and *Too Scared to Tell.*

# Introduction

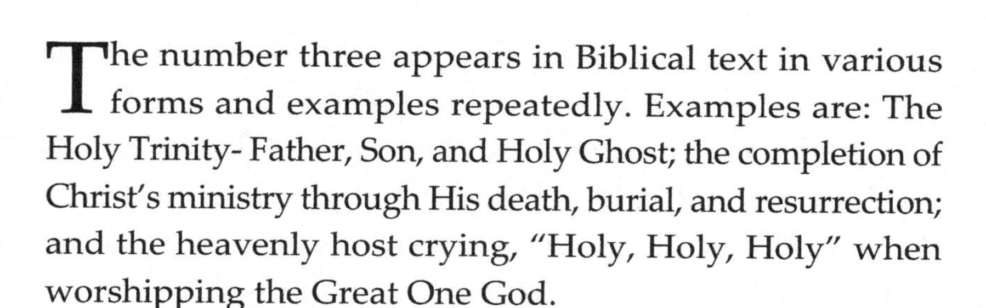

The number three appears in Biblical text in various forms and examples repeatedly. Examples are: The Holy Trinity- Father, Son, and Holy Ghost; the completion of Christ's ministry through His death, burial, and resurrection; and the heavenly host crying, "Holy, Holy, Holy" when worshipping the Great One God.

I could go on and on with the numerous times three is emphasized in the Scriptures. During my life, the number three attached validity in sequences of various trials and resulting blessings. I titled this book, *Always Three A Trilogy* because it contains three short stories which relate to biblical advice and admonitions. Each story provides examples and wise offerings to succeed in our earthly journey through biblical, spiritual reflections and warnings. Each of these stories provides individual forms of communicating principles for living biblical lives pleasing to God. The stories are, "Older to Younger-Let's Talk," "My Story of Three," and "Lilith the First Wife."

Humankind has interpreted the Word of God, the Bible, in numerous ways through their denominational connections throughout time. Interpreting and creating meaning to the unseen is the task of the last presentation, "Lilith the First Wife." Lilith has little recognition in many

Christian circles, yet according to research, she has a present earthly following.

Open forum questions from those under 50 years of age are answered from those 70 plus years old. The questions are about handling a variety of life's issues are addressed in the second story. "Older to Younger- Let's Talk." The second story, "My Story of Three" provides personal reflections of three life-changing events that came together within a three-month period during the same season.

"Older to Younger" and "My Story of Three" offers wisdom for daily living and triumphs from modern day calamities. Using biblical truths, and some fiction, God has allowed me to share his unfailing love, grace, provision, and strength. They are available during trials and temptations, and provide enduring triumphs for His children on planet earth. My prayer is that all who read these selections will come away knowing that God will bring you through every circumstance, past, present, and future.

# CHAPTER 1

## Older to Younger-Let's Talk

### (Relational & Rejection, Spiritual & Financial, and Racism)

There are hundreds of life issues you will face as you enter adulthood and progress to old age. Many possibilities have never entered nor crossed your mind. Perhaps you have looked at the life of an older person and wondered why this or that took place, or why do they live the way they do? Life scenarios are endless but those listed below are not designed to discourage you. They give you real-life situations and methods of survival through God's grace and mercy and the testimonies from the older generation.

These scenarios, questions, and admonitions were taken from true events in the lives of various people. You need not worry about your life but know that life can offer various unexpected and sometimes hurtful trials and challenges. But be of good cheer and courage, Jesus has overcome the world and hopefully you will receive encouragement from these brief writings and remember them as you age and grow in wisdom. May the Spirit of the Highest God through His Son, Jesus Christ, encourage and be with you by His Holy Spirit.

**Declarations:**

Psalm 78:4, NLT: "We will not hide these truths from our children; we will tell the next generation about the glorious deeds of the LORD, about his power and his mighty wonders." Amen!

Deuteronomy 4:9: "Only take care, and keep your soul diligently, lest you forget the things that your eyes have seen, and lest they depart from your heart all the days of your life. Make them known to your children and your children's children...." (ESV)

## Relational and Rejection

A divine opportunity came when I was asked to serve on a panel and speak to a select group of female graduate students at Southern University and A&M College in Baton Rouge, Louisiana. The University is my alma mater and provided a fertile field for inquisitions about what women might want their younger selves to know. I prayerfully decided that my presentation to them would ask one question: "What would you want your younger college self to know?"

Participants were provided paper and pen to write their replies and submit them without identifying themselves, if they so desired. They were also informed that their answers would be included in an upcoming publication. Concerns from most participants related to three "Rs": Relationships, rejections, and religion! The highest percentage of them being about rejection!

Rejection, that human experience that wreaks torment with emotional, mental, and sometimes physical existences. It leaves a person feeling in their minds that they are unvaluable, empty, unwanted, used, and tossed aside as worthless or less than others. Rejection can also lead to infrequent and diminished human interactions due to the disappointments leading to mistrust of further interactions. Isolation can be terrible if God has not designed it as a current season.

Remember, both Moses and Jesus had seasons of isolation (Moses in the mountain with God and Jesus in the wilderness of temptations). Most human beings love for others to love them back or accept them. When acceptance is not perceived and does not happen the way expected, rejection occurs. Rejection can happen in any social setting; from career to worship/church settings, to personal friendship and romantic/marital settings.

An evil act of rejection in the Bible occurred when Lucifer rejected God's rulership and dominion and envied the positions for himself. Secondly, Lucifer persuaded a third of the angelic host to follow him. Third and highest on his list is to continue to persuade humankind to reject God. Some might argue it was not Lucifer's rejection but the attempt to exalt himself above God. Lucifer's self-exaltation was not rejection, it was self-promotion above God's authority with the desire to become God. His self-promotion was an all or nothing devotion to his agenda he introduced to the heavenly. It was their choice. One-third of the heavenly host decided to follow him to eternal damnation. Lucifer became his followers' god. Simply put, that was eternal prideful arrogance and included the rejection of Almighty God as King.

What is the origin of rejection? Origins for many foundational human experiences are in the Bible.

Rejection entered the human spirit when Adam and Eve, through their rebellion and disobedience to God, left an emptiness and void for all humankind. (This would not have occurred had not Lucifer not rejected God, and his position wasn't terminated, and he wasn't reassigned to the realms of earth.) The human receptacle where God usually communed with them intimately was now empty. There was now a difference in the way they received from God.

Before Adam and Eve disobeyed, God was their friend and took care of their every need. They never experienced emotional or physical rejection, loneliness, lack, sadness, fear, physical discomfort, nor rejection, until they rejected God. God, realizing the weakness of his creations, created from the beginning of time, a plan to win humankind back to Himself for eternal fellowship. This would be done by sacrificing His only Son, Jesus Christ. By coming to God and accepting Jesus Christ, as Our Lord and Savior, we move away from our fallen nature personality and return to Him by His grace. Hallelujah! Still, because of the fallen state of humankind, rejection continue to happen in this life.

The responses and concerns expressed by these young women were from the receiving end of rejection. Answers and suggestions from the older panelists serving with me, shed light to the younger ones through their experiences.

When asked, "What you would want your college self to know?" the fiftyish year-old graduate student said, "When a relationship does not last, don't judge yourself on how the relationship is going."

I thought, *what does she mean by that*? Who would or should she judge? Is she in the relationship? Or maybe she is speaking of someone else as if she is looking on? Or maybe she meant, do not feel bad or judge or condemn yourself if the relationship is not going well. Relationships...can be extremely hard to make work sometimes. Whether relationships are friendships, romantic, marital, siblings, professional, or with church folks...all of them can sometimes be hard to achieve success, maneuver, and overcome.

After some group discussions, it was determined that she was speaking about herself. She would have told her younger self to not be too critical on herself when the relationship did not last. That was such an amazing observation for her younger self to know. It made me smile thinking about how gracious and caring God is to have imparted loving kindness in her heart. It allowed her to say something close to Scripture. His Word says, "Therefore, there is there now no condemnation for those who are in Christ Jesus..." (Romans 8:1). Our Father God can comfort anyone He chooses with glimpses of Himself and His Word even when a person does not really know the Word. Although this graduate student did not divulge her relationship with Christ at the time, it was a marvelous answer that she gave for her younger self to know. Take courage if you are in a younger self time, then, move on!

You do not have to condemn yourself when you learn to trust Christ Jesus. Ask for forgiveness, and begin to live life with freedom in Christ and move forward in a positive direction.

Moving forward can sometimes be difficult after broken relationships, like an unwanted change in careers. Or this can happen in relationships, like when divorce occurs. Pray and ask God in Jesus' name to help you stand on the promises of His Word. Declare with your words and ask God to help you understand how to apply to your unique situation, Philippians 3:13 states, "...but this one thing I do, forgetting those things that are behind, and reaching forth unto those things which are before, I press toward the mark for the prize of the high calling of God in Christ Jesus."

Moving on spiritually after a divorce might evaluate your strength and fortitude in church settings. Many church settings develop messages designed for married members. Single parents are generally given statistics of failure of children from single-parent homes, lack of success of single parents, and on and on. Disregard those messages and know that God has a good plan for your life. God did not fall off the throne when you went through a breakup or divorce. Continue to reach, and you must press on to the high calling which is in Christ Jesus our Lord! Failed relationships can be devastating when you wanted it to work. The failure often leads to difficulty to trust again even when a confidential ear is needed for support. Why? The ability to trust again due to relationship failure eliminates or decreases the concept of trusting others again! Or sometimes events might be aligned to end a relationship that was meant to be only for a season. Marriages are not seasonal or they should not be. Marriages are designed for permanence, but God knew there would be times that His beloved children would need to dissolve the commitment (unfortunately) legally. Read the words of Christ in Matthew 19:9 and Paul's admonitions in 1 Corinthians 7:10-17, Deuteronomy 17, etc. Always remember, study God's Word for yourself and learn to understand by His grace the full counsel of God. Never cherry pick verses.

Developing and securing trust involves the mutual upbuilding and time with unquestionable fidelity from both of the parties. When mutual upbuilding diminishes, it can yield catastrophic results with individuals or even member(s) of a group. The process begins with attempts to eliminate or discount one member in that group. Trust is lost by the affected individual, peace leaves, and that member is wounded and hurt. Now the hurt person becomes the victim. Heartache ensues and usually future relationships have a greater tendency for failure for that person/member(s). Why? The victim has been disappointed and builds a wall to protect him or herself from future rejection and hurt. That wall may even be subconscious, but it is still a wall that disallows true, meaningful connections because of past betrayals, rejections, and trauma.

This type of treatment is kindred to bullying. One member or person still desires acceptance but there seems to be nothing they can do to stop the rejection. If they continue to placate the treatment, their self-perception diminishes and bends to stay in the toxic environment/ relationship. This may sometime result in mental, emotional, and sometimes physical abuse. So, what can the victim do? The victim must pray and ask God for strength to move on and receive emotional healing while forgiving those who hurt them.

Many today might advise counseling as an option. Others would advise separation from bullying. Both are options to be prayerfully considered. What are peaceful characteristics of relationships? How can we achieve peace and build each other up? One way is to always be truthful with each other and try to determine what are the interest and uplifting ticks of the person(s) in the relationship. Be willing to be quiet and listen. We can learn the triggers that prohibit a lack of peace and not allow them to enter the relationship(s), whether they are friends or marriage prospects.

Before making a lifelong commitment in marriage, which involves lifelong trust, commitment, and compromise for the good of the marriage, there are a few things to be cautious about. During the dating phase, examine the triggers to see if there are red flag warnings to flee the relationship. Some triggers can show up as episodes of infidelity. Are they faithful and respectful before marriage? Let me explain. If a red flag or trigger of infidelity occurs, that means you might need to step back, look at the situation and call it off. Another trigger can be voice tone. Do you yell or talk too loudly? According to Proverbs 15:1, a soft answer/voice turns away wrath, but a harsh word stirs up anger. This can come across as anger or that you are attempting to be lord over someone (be that person's boss). In other words, you are yelling because you are in charge, and you believe you are the boss which might be a precursor to violence!

Exclusion also diminishes relationships. Of course, omissions or rejections are considered red flags or triggers. Do they elevate you or do you have to wonder if you are the only love interest? If you call them, do they recognize your voice or do they think you are someone else? That is a red flag. Did you or they forget to invite or include you or them to an event or activity and went on about your business as if it were not big deal? Did they exclude you from social settings while you were with them. For example, did you have to get a search party to locate them? When this type of behavior is repetitive towards a particular person (or group), there is a strong probability the relationship might be doomed to failure. It may not have been important to the person who forgot, but it meant something to the other person on the receiving end of the exclusion(s).

God wants our relationships to thrive in His love, holiness, and righteousness. Another more serious trigger could be confusion about the gender God assigned them, spiritual issues, and the lack of belief in Jesus as Lord and Savior. Christ love towards us is full and complete and He gives guidelines in His Word on how to walk in peace, love, holiness, and righteousness. Keep your word and understand that sometimes God might be allowing the separation of relationships. If that is the case, yield to God's leading and do not become entangled in the relationship. Do not become desperate. Prayerfully seek God, allow time for healing, and move on in peace.

*Let us Pray: Heavenly Father, thank You for the relationships you have assigned to my life at this time and season. I ask You for wisdom to discern how to build and promote peace, trust, holiness, and joy in all relationships whether friendly or romantic in hopes for a spouse. Help me know and understand when You are leading me out of a seasonal relationship(s). Help me to serve You and love You with all my heart in holiness with a good attitude. In Jesus' name, Amen.*

Two other young women had similar concerns. One was a former student of mine, and the other was a new acquaintance met during the conference. Below are their combined concerns.

1. "When learning to separate religion from relationship, what is one thing that was difficult to unlearn?"
2. "Will I ever complete something?"

The Scriptural foundations for both of the previous questions are 1 Corinthians 15:33 and Job 32:7.

1 Corinthians 15:33, ESV
"Do not be deceived: "Bad company ruins good morals"

Job 32:7, (NASB)
"I thought age should speak; And increased years should teach wisdom.'"

God used older people throughout the Scripture to provide wisdom and guidance to younger people. He used them even until they were incredibly old. God does not show respect of persons, that is, He will use whoever He wills. He uses the aged and the young. Just then, the forty-five-year-old shared her experiences as a teachable moment for those of mixed age groups to hear. God desires to use the older generation to help the younger generation. God used many older biblical characters to help provide wisdom and instructions to younger biblical characters. Their advice assisted them in successfully completing their purposes and assignments.

Examples of older people assisting the younger are Naomi and Ruth (*The Book of Ruth*), Mordechai and Esther (*The Book of Esther*), Eli and Samuel (*1 Samuel 3*), Moses and Joshua (*The Book of Exodus*), Paul, and Timothy (*1 Timothy 4:6*), etc. God is not a respecter of persons (*Acts 10:34).* God uses broken people, and some were young, and some were old people.

When asked what she wanted her college-age-self to know from her older self about leadership the forty-five-year-old said, "I want to tell my college self to complete something so I can say *well done* to myself. I went back to school at age forty-five and I believe I am a stronger leader because of it." She wanted her younger self to know that she could indeed complete something.

You do not have to be in your 20s or 30s to complete a college degree. From her deep heartfelt concern, I could see great remorse for what she felt was time lost. Always remember, if God gives you breath , it is never too late to complete your dreams or your something. God blessed me to complete and graduate with a Doctorate Degree at age 56. You are never too old. I read about a ninety-year-old woman completing her PhD program and her professors allowed her to write her dissertation by hand. You are never too old.

How do you begin to complete something? Prayerfully commit your daily dreams and plans to God. One day at a time. Write a plan, or if mental notes are better for you, do it! Whatever works best for you and your vision, but pray over it. Here are a few things you can do: Prayerfully ask God to send you help when needed. Help others with their dreams but helping them must not deplete your dream development time. Jesus set limits on His earthly time by telling His disciples His time was not yet, but they were always ready to do something! "Jesus said unto them, My time is not yet come but your time is always ready" (John 7:6).

Manage your time! Observe others who have succeeded in similar situations and if you feel you have the opportunity, ask them how they managed their time to complete their "something." Move forward and complete your something no matter how long it takes. God's grace is sufficient. If you have not been broken yet by life's trials, you might not be ready for your next step upward. These trials of brokenness bring experience, humility, understanding, and wisdom from God…when and if you are yielded and allow it. Be encouraged! Your time is coming for completion and God might allow some older person to give you some wisdom to help. Humility is the key to receiving help. Accept the godly wisdom and one day you will rejoice and say of yourself… "I completed it!"

One of my former students, who now owns her own business asked, "Can you separate religion from relationships? Is that possible?"

My answer is that depends on what you mean when you say "religion." Religion can be anything. A person can be religiously addicted to sweets, or a particular brand of cola. However, Christianity is faith and belief that Jesus Christ is the Son of God, and that God raised Him from the dead. It is a personal relationship with God through His son Jesus Christ and the Holy Spirit dwelling in our earthly temple. Our bodies are the temple of the Holy Spirit. I believe she meant Christianity. You may have non-Christian bosses/supervisors, co-workers, classmates, even relatives and acquaintances. However, it is possible to separate the two when it comes to close personal relationships. Remember, your life is now hidden in Christ and His Holy Spirit lives in you, and you do not want corrupt communications to spoil the good morals Christ has given you.

As a Christian, you cannot separate Religion or Christianity from relationships. Your faith in Christ Jesus makes you desire to live differently than those who do not have the same relationship. Your actions, words, decisions, etc., will sometimes conflict with those who are not Christian. Currently, much of society's moral standards do not abide by or even represent, resemble, or agree with God's moral standards. Sadly, some who call themselves Christians, have adopted the same worldly moral standards of today's culture.

Here is a list of current worldly standards that totally elude and mock God's Word and His desire for His children to live holy: abortions, male and female cohabitation without marriage or "shaking up," pre-marital sex, same sex-marital relations, same-sex ordination and leadership ordination in ministries, accepted profanity as normal in entertainment settings, on and on. Your life as a Christian is the guiding force to all your relationships and cannot be separated. Sharing the gospel of Jesus Christ to those who need to believe in Jesus as Lord and Savior is the mandate of Jesus. We are to go into all the world and make disciples. Once they are saved, prayerfully consider your future relationship with them as they grow in Christ. Remember, you are to lead, and their character should eventually show a sign of change towards godliness. Prayerfully determine if God wants you to become their mentor or if you are to guide them to a stronger mentor. Get godly counsel before you decide to become their mentor.

When you are committed to Christ Jesus and He becomes your Lord and Savior, He will, through His Holy Spirit, provide instructions for holy living according to His Word. When your life is yielded to Christ, the relationship with Christ takes top priority over all earthly relationships. None of us are perfect and that is why God sent Jesus to cleanse us by His blood and indwell us with His Holy Spirit. He will guide us into all truth while we live among fellow human beings. Christlike character is the guide in all relationships when you belong to God.

Never forget there is always forgiveness when sins are confessed through Christ Jesus our Lord and Savior for past and current sins. However, those who willfully continue to practice sin and are non-repentant should not be your bosom buddies. You are either in or out, especially when you know better. Willingly and deliberately betraying the one who died for your sins, means compromising your Christian testimony or Christian walk for an earthly relationship. When compromise is made for a relationship with an unbeliever or backslidden believer, you will become "unequally yoked."

The Word of God warns in 2 Corinthians 6:14, "Be ye not unequally yoked together with unbelievers for what fellowship hath righteousness with unrighteousness and what communion hath light with darkness?"

This phenomenon of being unequally yoked destroyed King Solomon's heart for true worship for God when he chose wives who did not worship God but rather other gods from their upbringing and origins. These unequal yokes led to the downfall of King Solomon's kingdom and his true worship of God. Hebrews 10:26 states, "For if we go on sinning deliberately after receiving the knowledge of the truth, there no longer remains a sacrifice for sins" (ESV).

**Prayer Point:** *Heavenly Father, you said in your Word that my steps are ordered by you throughout my life. Nothing takes you by surprise. I am asking you for wisdom and strength to complete my current assigned task You have allowed in my life and wisdom for all my current and future relationships. Guide me by the power of Your Holy Spirt in Jesus name on the correct path, assigned connections and relationships, and resources. I give You all the praise and glory in Jesus' name for keeping me aligned with your purpose for my life. Amen.*

John 16:13 states, "But when He, the Spirit of truth, comes, He will guide you into all the truth; for He will not speak on His own initiative, but whatever He hears, He will speak; and He will disclose to you what is to come." (NASB 1995)

The college student who was in her early twenties, said, "I want to trust my gut and know that I am enough and do not have to dim my light for anyone. Some people seem to not like it when my light shines, so they try to dismiss or diminish my accomplishments."

The Bible gives an example of a woman who was overlooked and demeaned after being used for her owner's benefit. Her light did shine for a little while when she gave birth to a son. This is the story of Hagar, an Egyptian slave girl belonging to Sarah, Abraham's wife. The Book of Genesis tells us that God promised Abraham an heir, but Abraham was old, and his wife, Sarah, was old and barren. The Bible says in Genesis 16:1–16; 21:8–21, Sarah, the owner of Hagar told her husband, Abraham, to sleep with Hagar so the barren owner could have an heir. Tradition would make the baby of Hagar and Abraham, the male heir of Abraham and Sarah, the rightful owner of the child and its mother.

In Genesis 16:3, we read, "So after he had lived in Canaan for ten years, his wife Sarai took her Egyptian maidservant Hagar and gave her to Abram to be his wife. And he slept with Hagar, and she conceived. But when Hagar realized that she was pregnant, she began to despise her mistress. Then Sarai said to Abram, "May the wrong done to me be upon you! I delivered my servant into your arms, and ever since she saw that she was pregnant, she has treated me with contempt. May the LORD judge between you and me." (BSB)

Some might call it Karma, but the Bible calls it you "reap what you sow." Is it not ironic that the descendants of Abraham served as slaves in Egypt for 400 years? That's the same nation of Hagar's origin, the slave who bore Abraham's first son, Ishmael. Why Egypt for 400 years? Egypt was immensely powerful at the time and had been made wealthy and prosperous by the godly wisdom and favor of Joseph the Hebrew. God wanted to show himself strong on behalf of His people by delivering them while simultaneously providing vengeance for Hagar's ill treatment. After all, there were many other nations that could have been used to enslave the Hebrew nation.

Hagar, the slave Abraham and Sarah tossed away, was allowed by God to make it. She made it after being tossed away by people who no longer had use for her after God blessed them with their own child. But God! God blessed

Hagar; the Egyptian woman raised Ishmael to become a great nation as God said he would. She was not around to see the strength of Egypt, but always remember, God speaks of seed, time, and harvest. In time, Hagar raised her son on her own without the assistance of Abraham. God told Abraham that He would establish His covenant through Isaac, and when Abraham inquired as to Ishmael's role, God answered, Ishmael has been blessed.

"And Abraham said unto God, O that Ishmael might live before thee! And as for Ishmael, I have heard thee: Behold, I have blessed him, and will make him fruitful, and will multiply him exceedingly; twelve princes shall he beget, and I will make him a great nation" (Genesis 17, 17-18).

In Genesis 25, 12-14 we read, "This is the account of Abraham's son Ishmael, whom Hagar the Egyptian, Sarah's maidservant, bore to Abraham. These are the names of the sons of Ishmael in the order of their birth: Nebaioth the firstborn of Ishmael, then Kedar, Adbeel, Mibsam, Mishma, Dumah, Massa…."(BSB)

God always has a good plan for all (Jeremiah 29:11), but He wants us to seek and obey Him. He wants us to become obedient even tough permitted sufferings and rejections may occur. Many times, rewards follow later.

Once I walked through a time of employment rejection which was emotionally and financially painful. However, hindsight given by God has shown me that had not rejection occurred, I may have never continued my professional education by earning a Doctorate Degree. That propelled my career, salary, and professional/

spiritual influence, and acquaintances. The point is, it might hurt, but God will bring you through with abundant blessings if you allow the process and keep God first.

**Prayer Point:** *Heavenly Father, I admit and ask Your forgiveness for going my own way in developing and seeking relationships. Help me and give me wisdom to discern and obey Your directions in the future. Let only Your will be done in all my closest connections including my future spouse and close friends in Jesus' name I pray, Amen.*

Matthew 10:19 states, "And whosoever shall not receive you, nor hear your words, as ye go forth out of that house or that city, shake off the dust of your feet. (ASV) Psalm 34:18 states, "The Lord is nigh unto them that are of a broken heart; and saveth such as be of a contrite spirit"(KJV).

These two verses provide comfort. The Lord is near the broken-hearted and provides direction for actions to take when you are not received. Even though Matthew 10:19 refers to sharing the Word of Life, it has also been used to define actions after rejection in a personal matter. An example of God showing himself near the broken-hearted is described in the life of Leah.

Leah, was the less attractive and older sister. Rachel, evidently had a contrite spirit because God looked upon her and favored her with many children. Leah was assigned by her father to marry a husband who never really loved her, and she never had first place love in Jacob's heart. Jacob loved Rachel more than her sister, Leah. Leah kept trying to be her husband's first love by praying to

God to bless her with more children for her husband. In their cultural norms, bearing children should have gained or given her more love or favor with her husband but it never really did. Leah never left but stayed in this normal cultural situation. She stayed and died in an unloved rejected state, yet she was proud of her accomplished childbearing. From these two examples we see how these women faired. It appears the most joy Leah ever had was the times she would hire Jacob to sleep with her and God would allow her to conceive again and bear more children. That is her fulfillment, and she was an obedient woman in the eyes of God. Her name and children are listed in the legacy of Jacob.

"And Dinah the daughter of Leah, which she bare unto Jacob, went out to see the daughters of the land" (Genesis 34:1, KJV).

"The sons of Leah; Reuben, Jacob's firstborn, and Simeon, and Levi, and Judah, and Issachar, and Zebulun:" (Genesis 35:23, KJV)

This story shows that things do not always turn out as we desire, but Leah became content with her status and situation. We can prayerfully decide which one we want to end up like. Fortunately, the cultural norms and laws of most states in the United States of America consider polygamy unlawful. Leah birthed seven children to Jacob. In today's western culture, Jacob's life would be considered a probable reason for criminal arrest and or divorce. Which brings us again to red flags. Do not forget, examples of red flags include lying and being untrustworthy in personal commitment to you, irresponsible with finances, jobless, lack of discipline or life goals.

In Jacob's case, he never loved you in the first place, but he followed the customs of the time. Do you have to wonder if they are being faithful? Are their finances in shambles or are they jobless? If these exist, please exit, and run away in the opposite direction! Heartache from betrayal sets you up for failure. You are better than that. Wait for God to send the right person. Please never overlook the red flags or believe you can change someone's behavior. It will be easier to move on now rather than later before the relationship becomes too involved and permanent.

Women often experience a life of rejection by a spouse while the world looks on and think that all is well. We must remember God knows we have been hurt and He still wants the best for us. We might not know how to let go or do not want to let go, even when the other person no longer wants a relationship. God will show you a way to receive a healed soul and spirit though His mighty power! This is the time to schedule seasons of "alone times of prayer" for courage and strength from God to continue.

Sometimes, additional godly counseling is necessary. It is also good to have a true, faithful, genuine friend (preferably female if you are female or male if you are male) that you can be open and honest with. We all need a friend who shares our faith and will keep our discussions confidential. Letting go can take time. It can be emotionally draining even when you are outwardly okay. Check up on yourself by setting goals to achieve your new emotional independence and celebrate as you improve by giving God all the praise.

Two other students asked:

"What do I do or how should I handle it when I have to let people go or they leave my life?" Or how do I let someone go who no longer wants to be a part of my life?"

"Many times, in life we wonder did I make the right decision? This is especially true when it comes to dating. What should I do? Who do I trust to share my heaviest burdens and dreams?"

Breaking the ties in relationships can be painful and difficult. Why? You have memories of social gatherings, verbal contacts, and affirmations and you long for the familiar. The problem is those gatherings, contacts, and affirmations no longer exist, and you attempt to recreate them, if only in your mind. Or you mourn for them as if you are mourning for someone is passing away. Something did pass away. The ties you previously had, have passed away. Take time to evaluate what you believe you are missing. You might not understand that you are missing the rejections, put-downs, etc. Now you have the time to see what was wrong the entire time and be set free by the power and grace of God in Jesus' name. It was what you thought you missed but never really had in the first place. The tie might have been one-sided all along. You were deceived.

Own it and ask God to give you His strength to move on. I heard a well-known female minister say, 10% of people will never like you. Just know, God always loves you and will never leave you.

Seasons in your life will change and some friends may not be your forever friends for assorted reasons. Do not despair. Learn to prayerfully determine your seasons of life. God is faithful to bring you through these experiences. Learn to trust Him. Jesus suffered rejection(s) by his "homies" in Nazareth where He couldn't do many miracles because they rejected His power. They were too familiar with His "homeboy" identity to accept His identity as Messiah and His power from God. Judas rejected Jesus and Peter denied Jesus. Therefore, Jesus is familiar with and acquainted with our griefs, rejections, and loneliness. The ultimate rejection for Jesus came when His Father forsook Our Lord to complete his divine destiny when he entered deaths door from the cross for my sins and yours. Jesus is acquainted with the rejections that His sheep experience. He went through rejection to be acquainted with our sufferings. Take time for yourself, prayerfully learn how to be alone for a while, until God guides you to new friends. He will in His timing. If this is a dating or romantic situation, other things need to be considered.

When you belong to Christ and confess your lifestyle as a Christian, much prayer should accompany the dating process. American culture differs from other cultures when it comes to dating. Many ungodly philosophies exist from cohabitating as married folks yet not married, to sharing expenses, living together, and making major purchases like homes, automobiles, boats, etc., as if legally married. Be aware, the justice system will not recognize the two of you as legal partners with "community property" status and neither does God. The Word of God does not honor or recognize your cohabitation as holy or legal. It is sin. Purpose to pray, seek godly counsel, and a security check…just kidding, but it might be needed when dating in the 21st century. Why? Fake or fraudulent online profiles, introductions, communications, and emotional ties with total strangers, occur daily.

Some people have been successful and have met "Mr." or "Ms." Right from an online experience while others, have not had much success. There are godly Christian guidelines and surveys in the cyber world and among some Christian ministries developed by godly people. The goal is to help you determine who might be worthy of your time and investment in developing lasting healthy godly friends and romantic relationships that lead to marriage. A little research or Google search for *godly surveys for dating and for friendly relationships,* and you will find an abundance of assistance.

Prayer, godly counsel, research, and the confirming peace of the Holy Spirit, will guide you in the right direction. And be cautious of those who do not seem to rejoice in your accomplishments. We are taught in God's Word to "rejoice with those who rejoice and weep with those who weep" (Romans 12:15). When a person cannot rejoice with you, you need to take a step back from their lack of encouragement. At least until you get a better understanding of the direction God wants you to take. Generally, it is away from that person. Take it slow and prayerfully do your homework.

"For we do not have a high priest who cannot sympathize with our weakness" (Hebrews 4:15, NKJV).

**Prayer Point:** *Oh Lord, can You see and feel the hollow I have in my heart? I have made every attempt, but nothing is working. Let your presence fill the empty spaces in my heart. Lead, guide, and give me wisdom to discern where I should be, who I should trust, and who my close associates should be. Only you know the heart and motives of every person. Help me to wait on you. In Jesus' name. Amen.*

**Prayer Point:** *Heavenly Father, your Word says you are a friend who sticks closer than a brother (Proverbs 18:24). Your word also says You will never leave nor forsake us (Hebrews 13:5). I need a friend. It seems I do not have many now and I do not know who to trust. Please be my best friend. Walk with me every day and show me where to go. Give me discernment to understand who a loyal friend might be and not be deceived anymore concerning fake friendships. Please show me how to become a true and better friend to others. I know you experienced all of this before because you had fake friends. Please help me. In Your name I pray. Amen.*

## Spiritual and Financial

### *Spiritual-Knowing God's Love and Salvation*

"And thou shalt love the Lord thy God with all thy heart, and with all thy soul, and with all thy mind, and with all thy strength; this is the first commandment... There is none other commandment greater" (Mark 12:30-31, KJV).

"That if thou shalt confess with thy mouth the Lord Jesus, and shalt believe in thine heart that God hath raised him from the dead, thou shalt be saved. For with the heart man believeth unto righteousness; and with the mouth confession is made unto salvation" (Romans 10:9-10, KJV).

"For all have sinned and come short of the glory of God" (Romans 3:23, KJV).

"Many are the affliction of the righteous, But the Lord delivers him out of them all." Psalm 34:19 (ESV)

Your utmost spiritual priority is to offer your life to God by believing in His son, Jesus Christ. Now we will first discuss the spiritual and the basis of why we need a Savior. Afflictions were not a human experience before the fall of man. Afflictions and trials are descended from the fall of mankind to sin and rebellion through Adam and Eve. Since that time, unwanted and sometimes, by choice afflictions and trials, come to all human beings at any age, station, and stage of life. The word afflictions in Scripture relates to having sorrows. There are all types of afflictions/

sorrows which might occur because of individual choices. God allows trials for growth. This includes self-allowed wrong influences from people who do not value your goals or principles of God's Word, and other various outside influences and people.

Possible afflictions and sorrows include injuries, illnesses, health and mental challenges, addictions, emotional, amoral, and immoral deceptions, negative finances, platonic and romantic stress, and spiritual struggles. These come from the fallen sin nature of man through Adam's and Eve's choice to ignore God's command and Word through disobedience by their submission to Satan. Their choice led to their separation from God's plan of eternal life for humanity and it affected every human seed that born of man and woman. That is why all humankind has a sin nature. We were all born as sinners.

Because God loved humanity, He in His mercy and grace, developed a plan to draw humanity back to Himself and deliver them from Satan. God sent Jesus Christ to pay the sin debt for all humanity. Jesus paid that debt by living a sinless life, being tempted as all humankind, yet not submitting to sin, dying on a cursed cross. He took on the sins of every human being who chooses to believe in Him. Jesus defeated death, hell, and the grave through His resurrection from the dead and His shed blood sacrifice, provided cleansing from all our sins. Those who choose to believe on Him can live for eternity in the Kingdom of God, a Kingdom without sorrows, weeping, sin, hatred, sicknesses, and death. A personal relationship with God through Jesus Christ is required to enter Heaven. You must believe in your heart and confess with your mouth that you believe Jesus Christ is the son of God and He died for your sins. Each day by God's grace, live a life pleasing to God according to His Word, the Holy Bible. God raised Jesus from the dead and Jesus is alive right now and praying for all of us as we choose to serve Him and shun evil. (John 17:20-26) He has given us extra help and power through His Holy Spirit.

The Holy Spirit is the comforter that guides us into all truth. Now, you can begin to live a life that changes your family and social relationships. Learn about biblical characters and examples through Bible study and prayer. Receive godly advice from true believers, pray and ask God to help you discern good from evil as described in the Holy Scriptures. Also fellowship with others who believe in Jesus as their Lord and Savior. Your new journey will involve your family and you will overcome by God's grace, mercy, the blood of the Lamb, and your testimony.

After you have surrendered your life to Jesus Christ, the Holy Spirit of God enters your spirit, it becomes new, and your name is written in the Lamb's Book of Life. (Revelation 13:8 and 21:27) You have a new eternal destination. A place where time no longer exists. A place where you will live forever in peace without sin, sickness, sorrow, and death. A place with God the Father, God the Holy Spirit, Jesus Christ our Lord and Savior, other believers, and the heavenly host. Hell is no longer your destination. However, before you leave earth through death or ascension through the great taking up, you will miss the mark of holiness or sometimes you will sin. You are still human and might lie, be envious, or whatever that goes against God's righteous lifestyle for His children. That is why you need to read and study the Bible for yourself. You will draw close to God by knowing His desires. Now, when you do sin, the Bible says in 1 John 1:8 states, "If we say we have no sin, we deceive ourselves, and the truth is not in us. If we confess our sins; He is faithful and just to forgive us our sins and to cleanse us from all unrighteousness. If we say we have not sinned, we make Him out to be a liar, and His word is not in us…."

God is always designing ways for repentance or turning away from sin. Confession they say is good for the soul. It is required for the believer to walk with Jesus free and clear of sin. Sinful ungodly cultural behaviors in the 21st century include demographically unbridled violence, mass shootings, hateful divisions within and without the Church, calling evil good and good evil, acceptance of immoral lifestyles, murders, abortions, and inhumane treatment of others because of their race.

How do you determine the right thing to do? You will know by prayerfully studying your Bible, surrendering your life to Christ Jesus, and asking God to reveal truth to your heart. You will then grow stronger in God and discern if truth is being preached in the sermons you hear.

Some ministries emphasize prosperity rather than righteous living. The Bible says, "For what shall it profit a man, if he shall gain the whole world, and lose his own soul? Or what shall a man give in exchange for his soul?" (Mark 8:36, KJV). Avoid those ministries if possible.

"...The word is nigh thee, even in thy mouth, and in thy heart: that is, the word of faith, which we preach; That if thou shalt confess with thy mouth the Lord Jesus, and shalt believe in thine heart that God hath raised him from the dead, thou shalt be saved" (Romans 10:8-9, KJV).

## Finding A Place to Worship

"Not forsaking the assembling of ourselves together, as the manner of some is; but exhorting one another: and so much the more, as ye see the day approaching." (Hebrews 10: 25, KJV)

Historically, the church in the New Testament Christian environment were small home group fellowships with family, friends, and other believers who loved the Lord Jesus. Worship at the Synagogue services included men and women who were separated from each other. Today, modern churches around the world include all people and all ages. What should you look for in a church? Answering that question is as simple as the Gospel. Jesus Christ the Son of God must be exalted in word, deed, and teaching. The way of salvation and holiness must be emphasized because the Bible says, "without holiness, no man shall see God."

Find a place to worship where the poor and needy are ministered to, has evangelistic and mission purposes, and does not exalt nor teach on political issues. Instead find one that teaches the Word and the love of God and does not make second class or no class Christian members out of any of its members.

Fellowship time with other believers inside and outside of the church house is important. Other important characteristic to look for when finding a church is holy worship that honors the name of Jesus and uplifts God's Word. It is especially important that the church observes the Lord's Supper or Communion, utilizes, and practice spiritual gifts, evangelism, the teaching of God's Word and baptism.

Assembling with others who believe in Jesus will help you become stronger in your relationship with the Lord Jesus. Sharing your life with Christ with other believers will also help you communicate the message to others who might need to know Jesus. Relaying the message will become easier as you share your testimony of what God has done in your life. Growth in your faith includes learning about your Savior through daily Bible reading and prayer. It is called fellowshipping with God through His Word. Select a version of the Holy Bible for your personal use that is easy for you to understand. Remember "forsake not the assembling of yourselves together" (Hebrews 10:25). This means as a believer, you will need to have continuous fellowship with other Christians in worship settings. This may also provide a setting for your testimony to encourage others. In today's culture, congregation size can range from small to mega-sized. Let the Lord direct you to where you believe He wants you to worship. Be faithful there until He guides you someplace else.

Prayerful consideration for choosing a place of worship should include the following questions: 1. Does the church follow the Word of God in its doctrine? 2. Does the church offer non-biased fellowship among all ethnicities? 3. Is it a full gospel church where the infilling of the Holy Spirit with the evidence of speaking in tongues, praying for the sick, laying on of hands, etc., is present? This is mentioned in the New Testament teachings of Christ according to the Books of Mark and Acts. Are all attendees treated with dignity as far as you can tell? Now, these are some things to be aware of. However, you must follow the leading of the Holy Spirit to find where He wants you to fit in for a designated season. Prayerfully consider your family (spouse, children, or other family members) when and if the Holy Ghost guides you to move on to another fellowship. As your walk with Christ continues throughout your life and service making a change sometimes happens. Be cautious about places of worship that emphasize politics and endorsements of political characters above the Word of God.

In American culture, the "it's my right" philosophy is exalted and has spilled over into some churches. This type of philosophy creates great division within the Body of Christ. Avoid a divisive person and Church. 1 Timothy says many false teachings would occur. Chapter 1 verse 9-11 says: "We realize that law is not enacted for the righteous, but for the lawless and rebellious, for the ungodly and sinful, for the unholy and profane, for killers of father or mother, for murderers, for the sexually immoral, for homosexuals, for slave traders and liars and perjurers, and for anyone else who is averse to sound teaching that agrees with the glorious gospel of the blessed God, with which I have been entrusted…."

This philosophy which they believe their life choices evolve completely around their US Constitutional rights and civil liberties, is a culture where God's principles are considered optional at best. The problem is some of these philosophies disagree with "love they neighbor as thy self." They believe trumps biblical teachings of love, holiness, honoring God and parents, humility, marrying the opposite sex and caring for others. The sad problem is several ills of the nation evolve from "my rights" constitutional jargon which excludes the teachings of Christ and God's ways for living a holy life. Here again, self and the liberties of the US Constitution and Supreme Court decisions reign as supreme authority over God's Word!

For younger folks (and anyone else), the first step to becoming a wise person is submitting to Jesus as your Lord and Savior. Your former desire to submit to the detrimental influence of the cultural norms will begin to wane. This will happen even when some of them are endorsed by many churches and/or the US Constitution. Some modern churches endorse sinful lifestyles in opposition to God's Word and justify their doctrines by saying, "Jesus loves and accepts everyone."

They are correct in saying that, but they omit that Jesus came to change everyone as well. He came to change us from the sin-laden individuals we were to humans who live in preparation to meet and live in the presence of a Holy God in eternity. These churches will not lead you closer to God but to the one who deceived Adam and Eve; Satan himself!

Jesus forgave and cleansed a woman found in the act of sin. Jesus asked the woman who was caught in adultery where were her accusers? She no longer saw them and said in John 8:11, "No, Lord."

And Jesus said, "Neither do I. Go and sin no more." In other words, we are by God's grace and mercy to leave the sin alone. We are not told to affirm sin, accept sin as an alternate lifestyle, or bend the rules. We are told to "repent and go and sin no more."

In today's world, technology offers Bible versions online via computer, tablets, cell phone, and other devices. There is always room in your life to have a personal hard copy of the Word of God, the Bible. Everyone needs a copy to hold in hand, read, turn the pages, and make markings when they need to.

Avoid assemblies that promote more flesh than Jesus and His Holy Word and Spirit. Such occurrences might include boastful comments about church accomplishments, down rating or belittling other assemblies, and church social cliques. Also, stay away from churches that do not teach the whole counsel of God's Word." Your purpose for assembling with other believers is to draw spiritual strength and encouragement from each other during a time of united worship of our Lord Jesus Christ. We share and hear the Word of God as preached, and bring the tithes and offerings to God's storehouse (your place of worship).

As you draw near to God and grow spiritually in Him, you will yearn to be water baptized. Seek counsel from the pastor of the church where God leads you and inquire about baptism. As your desires change from the inside out, you will begin a walk of holiness. A walk of holiness means you will separate yourself from things that were not pleasing to God in your pre-Jesus life. You learn what displeases God by prayerfully reading and studying the Bible. Many things that used to cause you afflictions and sorrows will supernaturally drop off. Other sins of your past may take longer to overcome. God's grace will give you the opportunity to become victorious as you gain holy ground and overcome the works of the enemy by the blood of the Lamb and the word of your testimony. One day you will share with others what God has brought you through, how He has changed your life, and how He is using you for His glory.

Experiencing a desire to serve or do something for God in various areas of talents and giftings is another longing the Holy Spirit will give you. Many call this your area(s) of ministry. God has given every human being at least one gift, usually more than one, that can be used for His service and Glory. There are all kinds of ministries. "And he gave some, apostles, and some prophets, and some evangelists, and some pastors and teachers. For the perfection of the saints for the work…" (Ephesians 4:11).

Other types of ministries include service to the poor, generosity, prayer selected areas of the fivefold ministry, serving in a local church in various areas and using the talents God have given you. Examples of various talents include administrative abilities, music, communications, mercies, and kindness, etc. Ministry is not always confined to the inside of the church walls. During your personal prayer time, you will experience a nudge or desire from the Lord to serve in specific area(s). Continue to pray. God will open a door for your ministry gift. You will need to wait for the appropriate door to open. Always remember, your choices, even in ministry areas can affect your time with family. Be sure to have all things peaceful and in agreement in your home while you fulfill your ministry areas. Do not become discouraged. Do not restrain God or put Him in your own little box with your preconceived expectations of which door He will open. Do not attempt to force a door to open. Make yourself available to God without insistence. Be sure to humbly enter doors of opportunity because you are representing the King of Kings and Lord of Lords.

Just a little warning; do not allow ministry titles to go to your head. Many individuals add a litany of spiritual titles to their names. Some titles are "First Lady," "Prophetess," "Apostle," "Pastor," "Evangelist,"etc., and will demand to be addressed as such or you will be considered disrespectful or in rebellion. Many of these titled people in ministry do not address others outside of ministry with their titles and even make fun or demean their accomplishments. The Bible says do the same for others as you would have them do for you! That's called the Golden Rule, and is found in Luke 6:31 and Matthew 7:12. Stay humble, pray for them, trust God and wait for His specific door.

God will provide His strengthening power as you mature to move forward in your walk with the Lord. "The Lord is my strength he has given me victory...." Exodus 15:2 New Living Translation (NLT) Your personal relationship with God through prayer and personal Bible study, should always remain a daily part of your life. Pray and ask the Lord to fill you with the Holy Ghost with the evidence of speaking in tongues as in the Day of Pentecost in Acts Chapter 2. True and genuine fellowship with trusted Christians and God's great comforter, the Holy Spirit, will serve to help you grow in God's will. "But the Helper, the Holy Spirit whom the Father will send in My name, He will teach you all things, and remind you of all that I said to you" (John 14:26, NASB).

The Holy Spirt is the comforter Jesus said He would send. The Holy Spirit is the Spirit of God and Jesus Who will dwell in us forever when we accept Him as our Lord and Savior. He will provide for you based on God's Word, encouragement, peace, and joy in times of stress. Jesus' presence will become familiar as daily you become closer to Him as you learn to lean on Him through the trials and afflictions of life. Goodness and mercy will follow you daily. Your character will become Christlike, and you will bring more compassion in your dealings with others and hopefully receive more godly wisdom as well. The Holy Spirit will provide courage for you to share with others about how God brought you through various trials, the joy you experienced through them, and how He can do the same for them.

When you do this, you are applying the Word of God to your life, when it says, "they overcame him by the Blood of the lamb and the word of their testimony" (Revelation 12:11). "Many are the afflictions of the righteous, but the Lord delivers them out of them all" (Psalm 34:19).

Remember and understand that your life or walk as a Christian will not be without troubles, trials, disappointments, rejections, sickness, etc. You will also have blessings and many triumphs by God's grace. In other words, your life as a Christian will not be a bed of roses, a fairy tale, or without complications. Jesus, God's son, experienced every emotion and temptation any human could have and yet He was without sin. He did not yield to temptation and sin. Jesus encountered trails with His close followers, His disciples (Peter, Judas, Thomas, and the Sons of Thunder, James and John), and religious leaders (Pharisees, Sadducees, the Sanhedrin). You will too. Church trials can show up anytime. Jesus triumphed over these sins and temptations so that when we believe on Him and asked Him to become our Lord and Savior, His compassion and triumphal experiences would give us the ability to move forward and have victory in His strength. Be of good cheer, Jesus overcame all these trials just for you because He loves you. There will be blessings, miracles, and comfort from the Holy Spirit when you need it.

In your attempt to please God you will learn to accommodate expectations in your local church. If ever, God forbid, that your church is in error (teaching acceptance of ungodly lifestyles in the guise of loving others, cover ups of sin, etc.) quietly leave. Seek God through prayer and find another place to fellowship. Always remember, if you are not in charge of an organization you do not make the decisions. You do not have the option of making final decisions for your church as well as your place of livelihood when you are not in charge. You must comply or leave. When you leave, do so peacefully and without causing turmoil. If illegal or criminal matters exist and you are involved, seek legal counsel. Prayerfully allow the Holy Spirit to guide you to a place of worship where the Word of God and the name of Jesus is exalted above ministry and local celebrities. A place where prayer needs and concerns for members are important, making disciples of Christ is practiced, and teaching the whole counsel of God though Biblical constructs is magnified.

Church offences vary from the miniscule "stepping on your toe," to the thunderous sexual abuse. When offences occur, you might feel guided to worship and serve someplace else. Do not forget, you are dealing with another human being who needs grace like you. However, this does not mean you must become a doormat for offences. Avoid these types of social misbehaviors because your desire is to grow in Christ's love and serve Jesus. Enjoy fellowship with other loving believers while removing yourself from non-repentant ill treatment. The Apostle Paul encourages believers in 1 Corinthians 1-16 to love each other and get along. Unless God is allowing you to go through this for season, do not remain. Your goal is to seek peace and pursue it.

Always practice forgiveness and do not allow your peace or joy to be taken. Develop a way to keep your personal space and boundaries and remember Whose you are. You belong to Christ, and you are a new creation in Christ Jesus forever and no one can take that away from you. Prayerfully seek God on your place or purpose. Let

God's Holy Spirit guide you to a position of service for service in His Kingdom. Keep a clean heart and the joy of the Lord. Remember, you will have to give an account to God for your own decisions. It is important to include and obey God in your decisions even when you do not understand completely. After all, you belong to Christ Jesus, and you are His servant, not the ministry's servant.

"If your brother sins against you, go and tell him his fault, between you and him alone. If he listens to you, you have gained your brother. But if he does not listen, take one or two others along with you, that every charge may be established by the evidence of two or three witnesses. If he refuses to listen to them, tell it to the church. And if he refuses to listen even to the church, let him be to you as a Gentile and a collector" (Matthew 18:15-17, ESV).

If, God forbid, there is a scandal in your church or denomination and it becomes public media knowledge, do you remain and continue to serve and fellowship with that ministry? Or do you leave and pray to find another place to worship? There are many church and denominational scandals today! Follow the same process for this as in all other decisions you will need to make on your spiritual journey with the Lord. If you have family, be sure include them in your decisions. You might even get inquiries from those who do not attend your church or friends who would like to know the scoop about the scandal. Say absolutely nothing and mind your own business. Make sure by God's grace that you are not a part of the scandal. Prayerfully examine what the media says and what your church leaders say. Then weigh what you believe to be facts, asking God to give you His wisdom and guidance. Forgive those in the scandal, always asking God in the name of Jesus to keep your heart clean . Follow the leading of the Holy Spirit and do what He prompts you to do.

Discussing this with others is not wise. If you must confide in someone, make sure it is a spiritual mature person who will not tattle your concerns. If you cannot find a mature person or do not know one, connect with one of the reputable national Christian ministries that have a toll-free prayer line. A prayer partner will pray with you about your concerns, and you can remain anonymous and not share your location, etc. Scripture references teach how to handle offenses, insults, etc. One of the main teachings from the Lord Jesus is to forgive seven times seventy times if your brother offends you. You must forgive. However, it does not mean you cannot remove yourself from frequent and habitual offenses. As much as possible follow peace with all people.

**3 Financial**

"Bring the whole tithe unto the storehouse, so there may be food in food in My house (God's House), and put Me to the test now, in this, Says the Lord of armies, "If I do not open for you the windows of heaven and pour out for you a blessing until it overflows" (Malachi 3:10, NASB).

**Question:** Concerned about her future and how to manage her finances/money, the University student asked: "What is the most effective way to manage my finances when I'm older and have my career? And how do I let someone go who no longer wants to be a part of my life? How do I live without thinking about the 'what ifs'?"

**Answer**: Remember, the past is just that, the past! You will always have the past, present, and future. The past is over, the future is not here yet, and you are only living in your present. Your "what ifs" can stagnate you or provide cautious wisdom. You must learn to pray for wisdom to choose correctly and ask someone who is godly their thoughts on your situation. Whoever you ask must be trustworthy and possess godly wisdom. You do not know the future so you must trust that God has good plans for your life. God's plans are good and not evil. His plans give you hope, and a future (Jeremiah 29:11). God will provide wisdom to discern what is absolutely necessary at each stage of your life. Make sure you tithe and your financial budget and planning over the years includes proper insurance for medical, residential (buying or rental) insurance, automobile insurance, life insurance for any heirs and your final expenses. (Your departure from this planet into eternity—your funeral). Make sure you take loving care of yourself by having regularly, scheduled physicals, dental, eye, and special medical gender specific checkups (mammograms and pap smears/women and prostate/men, etc.) as well as affordable vacation breaks.

As you age, it seems less is needed to survive. There is less shopping for career clothing (you should have a closet full of clothes by the time you are near retirement age), and by the time you retire, you should have a place to live (hopefully with all furnishings and the mortgage paid off). You should also have a stable vehicle that will carry you for several years and an attitude and aptitude of gratefulness to spend wisely. By God's grace and mercy, maintain your finances and credit worthiness by not having to file bankruptcy for not meeting your financial obligations in a timely manner. I am not condemning anyone who may have had various financial trails, but I am suggesting that anyone can make a turnaround. Start managing your finances through budgeting, saving, and spending wisely. By the time you are 50, preferably before 40, you should have a steady financial base, especially for emergencies.

God can and will use godly wisdom from those who have already triumphed in their finances to help you with your planning if you ask for help. Humility on your part is the key. When an individual no longer wants to be a part of your life there is usually no way to persuade them otherwise.

There is a Biblical story in 2 Samuel 13. King David had a son named Amnon. Amnon had a half-sister named Tamar. Amnon lusted for Tamar terribly and he raped her. After he raped her, he hated her. "No sooner had Amnon raped her than he hated her—an immense hatred. The hatred that he felt for her was greater than the love he'd had for her. 'Get up,' he said, 'and get out!'" (2 Samuel 13:15, MSG).

This example is used to show how sometimes what people think is love is actually lust. This leads to sexual sin and one partner is left hurting because the other partner was not in love but rather in lust and discards them. Humble yourself and ask for help. Trustworthy experts can show you where to invest your time as you heal from the rejection of people or someone who no longer shows an interest in being a part of your life. Prayer and receiving wisdom from God and godly counsel will guide you in successful movement to your God-designed purpose. God desires joy for all His children. Your body should be saved for marriage and be shared with one person, your marriage partner. There is forgiveness for any sin through Jesus. One person cannot stop your joy. Allow God to heal you. Move on and learn to build trust in those worthy of your trust.

Learn to trust that you have heard from God when you decide you not to be plagued with the "what ifs." For years, I prayed and asked God to meet a desire I had for becoming debt free. God began meeting that need though a purchase made at a thrift sale. Lo and behold it was unbelievably valuable and I was able to use the profits to eliminate several bills. Did you notice, I did not say that I was able to splurge and have my nails done, etc. Take seriously the business of finances. I never expected to run into something like that, even though I had prayed to become debt free, and I paid my tithes on the increase. What I learned from that experience is, not to cramp God's style or put Him in a box. God met a need in an unorthodox way. Allow God to have His way. We can never really figure it all out.

Which brings me to this point. Since God can show up in unusual ways, keep your expectations high and follow the Holy Spirit's promptings. Another especially important point is that God honors His word. He was "rebuking the devourer for my sake" after He allowed me to bring the whole tithe (10% of my salary) for years, even during extreme financial needs. That lasted for at least 25 years. I never lacked daily health and living provisions, home, food, transportation, and necessities for my two children. However, I still had debts I wanted to eliminate. Suddenly, an unexpected abundant downpour of finances came and helped to eliminate all my large bills. Later, I totally became debt free. I didn't have a mortgage, car note, nor credit card payments. God is faithful to His word. The testimony of that downpour of blessings can be seen on a CBN testimonial video listed in the references.*

"God answer you on the day you crash, the name God-of-Jacob put you out of harm's reach, Send reinforcements from Holy Hill, Dispatch from Zion fresh supplies, Exclaim over your offerings, Celebrate your sacrifices, Give you what your heart desires, Accomplish your plans" (Psalm 20: 1-4 1-4 MSG)

**Question:** "What is the greatest wisdom you ever received and how can you apply it to your life and share it with others?"

**Answer:** "Think Cheryl, Think!" is a quote my dad that would always say to me.

My mother's constant reminder was, "Don't let your feet drag or your head hang down."

The quotes from my dad, the late Rev. Tipp M. Major Sr., and from my late mother, Mrs. Allie Payne Major, have stayed with me all my days. At seventy-four years old, I still hear in my spirit and abide by those words.

One example of utilizing the first quote of wisdom was when I first became head-of-household through abandonment and divorce. I used my home equity to lower the mortgage payment and receive extra cash after my husband deserted and abandoned, then divorced me. I voluntarily inherited the marital debt (including the mortgage that placed the family home in my name).

My desire was to keep my children in their familiar normal domicile. Later, I thought, just like Daddy said. Those thought processes helped me plan and strategize how to make my budget more fluid with extra cash and one salary by taking on part-time jobs that allowed me to work from home and be with my young children. These "thinking" thoughts yielded plans and strategies to be content with what I had. Yet, they allowed me to stretch every dollar that the Lord provided to become debt free, travel and have free or low-cost vacations with my children. I used credit cards to my advantage by charging monthly expenses on a card that provided points for hotels and gift cards, etc. It was easy to do because charges were included in my budget (utilities, insurances, taxes, tithes, etc.). Eventually in 2016, God allowed me to totally become debt free. Praise His Name!

The second wisdom came from my mother's lips. There are people who do not mind making you feel bad or attempt to bring you down a notch because they do not like what God has allowed you to accomplish along your journey. They never stop to think about the trials and struggles you may have experienced achieving whatever accomplishment(s) they hate dearly.

Years ago, while I was still a youth, I read a Scripture in the Bible like Momma's statement: "You won't see us drooping our heads or dragging our feet! Cramped conditions here don't get us down" (2 Corinthians 5:6, MSG). I wonder did she know that her statement to me was a near perfect quote from 2 Corinthians? There were opportunities for embarrassment, rejection, and ostracizing moments during my younger days as well as adulthood. You will have them, too. We all have opportunities for our heads to hang down and our feet to drag. For me it was from personal insults directed at me as a chubby girl in elementary. As I grew up, the weight came off. You might say I loss some baby fat and became an athletic teenager. Adulthood brought on heavier rejections and ostracizing.

Then, when Daddy died a new or different type of hurt evolved. Grief. My mother saw the hurt in my eyes from an incident and she would always say, "Don't you ever let your feet drag or your head hang down." Then she would encourage me in my areas of strength and make me smile with my head up before the conversation ended. You see, having your head down and your feet dragging meant you were walking slowly without enthusiasm, without purpose, or without a take charge spirit! You were sad, embarrassed, or in today's vernacular depressed. Momma taught me to look up and remember what God had placed in my heart and spirit and walk with a high step. God will lift your head through all mishaps. He is the glory and the lifter of your head! Devastations, embarrassments, illnesses, and all kinds of trials in this life may come. Remember, you serve and love Jesus who loves you and has overcome them all for you. I can share that God is faithful to send activities to help you overcome all rejections and other people to help you enjoy the days He has given you.

> "But thou, O Lord, art a shield for me; my glory, and the lifter up of mine head" (Psalm 3:3, KJV)

**Question:** "Why is it necessary to honor older folks? Sometimes I just wish they would get out of my way."

**Answer:** Younger folks have had grandparents who offered loving care and wisdom to them, and they respect and adore them and their memory. However, in many cases, younger people want older folks to sit down and stay out of their way. The question is, how will you manage this when *you* the younger, are the older? Will you become offended? Will you retaliate? What will you do when a younger one comes to you and requires you to disappear into the background? Or do not honor or listen to your wisdom or advice? Or kick you to the curb?

A female teacher once discussed an incident with a female high school student. The teacher saw the student being fondled near the school cafeteria during lunch break by a male student. When the break ended, the teacher had a private conference with the female student and advised her that the behavior was inappropriate. She told her it could lead to undesirable consequences such as teen pregnancy. The student went home and told her mother about the teacher's conversation. The parent wanted the teacher to receive a reprimand because the mother said it was none of the teacher's business to speak to the girl about that kind of behavior. Really? Seriously? Public fondling? The teacher did not receive a reprimand but apologized and promised to never advise the young girl again. The teacher said she would not say anything to that student again even if the student was outside naked with the guy. Unfortunately, the young girl did not return for the spring semester.

Prepare yourself because this type of rejection could come from your business partner, coworker, or the church. Church offenses can be dark. They are dark because nobody wants to admit, or bring to the light, that they are offended, and the offender believes they are right and did not offend. Prayerfully seek God's direction for you next actions. Where would He have you to go or do? After all, you have been asked to stay back and most times you feel it is because of your age. God will guide you and give you fulfillment someplace else. You might suffer emotional hurt that might take a while to heal, but it will heal.

I read a post on FB that quoted a pastor. It said, "You need to know when to retire from the usher board and the choir." I also read on a FB flyer announcement from a church leadership for auditions for praise and worship singers with the age requirements of 25-45. Too bad if you are over 45! Is it because of age that you retire from ushering or the lack of the ability to function as an usher? Are you not cool enough to sing in raggedy jeans if you are over 45 years old?

1 Chronicles 25:8 states, "The musicians were appointed to their term of service by means of sacred lots, without regard to whether they were young or old, teacher or student." Moses did not retire until 120 years of age. Neither did his mentee, Joshua, retire early. Tony Bennet, during the time of this writing, was an exceptionally smooth-voiced world-renowned singer. For those too young to know who he is, he died in July 2023, at age 95. He still sang beautifully, even though he had memory challenges when he doesn't sing. His singing never failed him. What is the problem? Age discrimination in church is wrong, period!

Is it that older folks cannot communicate in younger folks' language? Is it that older folks do not appreciate younger folks' mannerisms or appearances? There needs to be a balance. Young people always remember, seeds you plant might become an exceptionally large produce in your life later. That produce will be either sweet or terribly bad and bitter fruit. Some of you might say, "I don't care." When following the Lord Jesus and desiring to be more like Him, it does matter. It never hurts to be kind and respectful to older people. Besides, those older folks have experiences they can share with you that may clear up unanswered questions you might have in areas of your life.

**Question:** "I am still young, why should I even think about retirement?"

**Answer:** Do you realize how swiftly the years of life will breeze by? Before you know it, you will be in your early fifties? If you are blessed to have children, they often leave your nest right before your career ends through retirement. The next thing you know, your entire daily schedule will change and the amount of income you normally spend on your offsprings will hopefully decrease. Your monthly income in retirement will be less than your normal take home pre-retirement salary. You will need to prepare yourself to live on less by having fewer outgoing expenses.

Ideally you should pay off large payments like your home mortgage and car payments before you retire. Revisit and update your budget to accommodate your new and smaller monthly retirement salary. You also want to manage expenses to include provisions for vacations or trips and outings that are affordable, and final expenses for your burial one day.

Biblically manage your finances. A comment on social media said, "If I knew life was going to be like this I would have started saving for retirement in kindergarten!" Honor God by paying your tithe as the Bible says and God will give you wisdom to spend and save frugally.

"Bring all the tithes into the storehouse so there will be enough food in my Temple. If you do," says the LORD of Heaven's Armies, "I will open the windows of heaven for you. I will pour out a blessing so great you will not have enough room to take it in! Try it! Put me to the test!" (Malachi 3:10, NLT)

Some older folks (like me) suggest tithing 10% and saving 10%, even during retirement years. The remaining 80% should be able to cover all other expenses (housing, utilities, transportation, insurances, and extra savings for vacations, entertainment, etc.). Are you willing to adjust your taste to your budget? Are you willing to prayerfully seek God about your expenditures? Are you willing to utilize gently used items if you have expensive taste in clothing, etc.? Are you willing to do your own fingernails and save the money?

It is good to seek trusted godly counsel if you feel unsure about handling your finances. While still involved in your career, it would be wise to have six months living expenses (including your rent/mortgage, transportation, life insurance, etc.) in savings reserve just in case you are unemployed for a season.

**Question(s):** "What will personal relationships be like when you are older? If you marry what if you survive your spouse? What if your spouse is no longer in your life? What if you never married? Will you still have those lifelong friends from your younger years? Will they still be your friends, or will God need to adjust your emotional mentality and relationships?"

**Answer**: Fortunate and blessed you are if you have the same best friend for life. Many times, this does not happen. Seasons come and go and so do relationships. Do not fret; you will always have a friend that sticks closer than a brother. His name is Jesus, but we also love to have friends in the earthly realm. Always remember Jesus suffered heartaches and betrayals by his close companions and like Jesus, your heart can suffer hurt when friends disappoint you. Forgive them and allow the Lord to heal your hurts and add new friends to your life who have the same or higher convictions than you. Allow a time of refreshing through a season of solitude. Prayerfully evaluate yourself and ask God to show you why the friendships ended. Ask someone you trust for an honest opinion and pray about it to prevent the same mistakes from happening again or becoming continuously repetitive. Some people suggest that you can only have one or two besties.

A good biblical account of best friends would be David and Jonathan. Read about it in 1 Samuel 18. Good friends do not backstab or speak ill of their friends no matter what has happened. Grief is another type of sorrow. Have conversations with a widower (if needed) to discuss with her how she managed the death of her husband or a divorcee about her life after divorce.

The bottom line is some of your friends' time on earth might end before your time is up. You will miss them terribly. I often feel sadden for individuals left behind when a spouse dies. If it was a good marriage, I am sure the loss is tremendous. If your spouse dies, you will have a different kind of singleness than persons who lose a spouse through divorce. Widows and widowers are often left in the old folks' singles group. They no longer have frequent companionship with those remaining living couples they hung out with before their spouse transitioned to heaven.

When singleness happens during the older years, connecting with reputable and safe senior groups for recreational activities and wholesome biblical fellowship is a good idea. You are still alive and should have fun during your remaining years. There are all kinds of special interest senior groups available that range from dancing, sports, travel, and knitting. Prayerfully and safely enjoy life. Some church congregations might have a monthly activity for older folks.

**Question:** "What do I do with my dreams that are not completed yet as I get older (travel, investments, relationships, ministry)?"

**Answer**: Prayerfully continue pursuit of your dreams if you are physically, mentally, and financially capable. Your body and health can endure more events when you are younger than when you become a senior or 55 plus. Whatever it is you desire to do, be about doing it before you are older. Years and life can slow your physical body down after wise and unwise use. The Bible speaks of Moses being strong at 120 years old (Deuteronomy 34:7), and Joshua (Joshua 1:9) and Caleb (Joshua 14:11) in their 80s. And they were still strong! Remember, in biblical times, most people walked as a means of travel unless they owned camels, donkeys, or horses. We should all believe God will help us to live wise, physically active, emotionally, and nutritionally sound lives.

The aging process for some people limits how fast they can complete some normal tasks, both physically and mentally. Extra help is sometimes needed or just learning to accept the fact that completion might take a little more time than usual. Attitudes as well as emotional adjustments are sometimes needed. Prayerfully seek God on when and what to do in preparation for your aging body. Do you need to downsize or move-in with relatives or adult children? Allow yourself to take advantage of annual physical medical checkups. If you are physically and mentally able to take on adventurous and challenging travels, then do so. Hopefully, your most adventurous life will occur while you have great strength and resources.

Preparation for finances for aging should begin while you are young by living beneath your means while maintaining an acceptable credit score. "An excellent credit score is 800-850, a very good credit score is 740-799, a good score is 670-739, a fair score 580-669 and below 579 is considered poor"—Experian.com. You earn an excellent credit score by making wise and necessary purchases, responsible spending, timely bill paying, and spending within your means. That is, make your purchases adhere to the income you earn. Plan for your retirement as soon as you begin your first full-time job. Prayerfully, your employment will afford medical and retirement benefits. If not, be sure to start early by investing in a retirement plan. Seek sound financial advice from an expert or someone you trust who has successfully managed investments. Create interest bearing saving accounts for yourself and your children's education. Make a Will. Begin to think and plan for your final arrangements as soon as you can afford it. There are long range plans available that can help you complete pre-arrangements for final arrangements so you can live your life without worry. Pray about where you might live during your senior years.

You might wake up one day and your limbs do not move as fluidly or as swiftly as before. People tire more easily as they begin to age. This is all a part of aging. Possibilities of aging are described in Ecclesiastes 11. This passage offers wise counsel on the seasons of life.

> "Oh, how sweet the light of day, And how wonderful to live in the sunshine! Even if you live a long time, don't take a single day for granted. Take delight in each light-filled hour, Remembering that there will also be many dark days And that most of what comes your way is smoke. You who are young, make the most of your youth. Relish your youthful vigor. Follow the impulses of your

heart. If something looks good to you, pursue it. But know also that not just anything goes; You must answer to God for every last bit of it. Live footloose and fancy-free—You won't be young forever. Youth lasts about as long as smoke" (Ecclesiastes 11: 7-8, MSG).

**Prayer Point:** *Lord God, as I look to my elder years, You know my desire to be faithful in all things. You also know that I have not managed my finances according to Your Word and promises. Today I ask You to forgive me, give me wisdom and courage to trust You with my finances. I want to tithe and save so that when You allow me to become an elder, I will be prepared. I cannot afford to give the entire 10% right now but I want to start with ___%. As you bless me, I will increase to 10% and faithfully bring You the whole tithe to your storehouse. In Jesus' name. Amen.*

**Question:** "I know it is scriptural to think on those things that are lovely, pure, and good report. But many of us really do not prepare for the unexpected. What should we do when the unwanted unexpected occurs and my thoughts run wild?"

**Answer:** Have you ever spoken with an older person and asked how they may have managed a specific devastating situation? Job loss, ministry failure, illness, debunked marriages, failed romantic and or friendly relationships or a children gone astray? Seeking help from those who have "been there, seen that, and done that before" will certainly help you gain some knowledge and possibly much wisdom for handling your specific situations. A word of caution: there are some older folks who are plain "perfect." Their possible boasting of their successes might make you feel worse than you did before you approached them. It is imperative you prayerfully seek out a compassionate godly person for advice. Ask them how they managed their thoughts during their situation(s)?

If you make your inquiries to a godly person about your unexpected events during your journey through life on earth, God may help you understand various trials of life through their testimony and counsel. One thing for sure, you will or you should increase empathy and compassion towards others in situations like yours. Some people have no desire or see the need to find out or seek life's wisdom from. This can be a serious problem. Their admonitions come from years of observations and life experiences. Their admonitions should bring understanding to Biblical truths and encouragement. Hopefully, younger people will carry some of this wisdom with them for their current or future life. Young people might be able to help a younger person later in your older life. You will be old one day.

**Prayer Point:** *Lord, Your word declares that You will keep me in perfect peace when my mind is stayed on You. I need Your help to do that. I have a full plate of distractions and I ask You to teach me how to focus on Your promises of provision, love, and wisdom. That will allow me to move on successfully with my life as I age. Help me to help others when I am young and old with godly wisdom when I can do so. In Jesus' name. Amen.*

### *Quick Points on Aging to the Younger:*

### *Lagniappe (a little extra) Tips*

1. If you live long, you will grow older and one day become the old man or woman in life's pages. Are you prepared for that day?
2. Facial aging might occur when you get that first facial smile crease around your mouth in your 30s. That is the beginning of facial aging for most. You wake up one morning, see a skin indent or crease/line where you have not seen one before.
3. You are more than your physical looks! Create godly character through your faith in God through His Son, Jesus and always know that you are fearfully and wonderfully made.
4. Sometimes 20/20 vision begins to change. You might need contacts or glasses to read "up-close" print.
5. If you had a muscle or joint injury during your teen years and it is healed during your 20s and 30s, it may reappear as you age. This could be in your late 40s and upward.
6. Learn to live within your financial means. Do not spend money to keep up appearances or attempt to outdo someone else. Learn to be content with what you have. Example, get a sofa throw instead of purchasing an expensive sofa if you cannot pay for it in cash. Do your absolute best to not create lingering and revolving debt. Fix up what you can,

economize and save using a budget. Prepare to have monetary resources during your senior years.

7. Save money for a rainy day. Start with what you can and watch it grow. Some savings are better than no savings.
8. When friendly relationships prove detrimental to your mental, physical, emotional, and spiritual well-being, do not be afraid to distance yourself. With the love of Christ, sever the relationship. God will send those you need in your circle for the time being.
9. Many friendships are seasonal. They are non-threatening but there for a season.
10. Follow your peace and the guidance of the Holy Spirit. Aging is a time where you need your strength to care for loved ones and yourself. Unnecessary turmoil must be avoided.
11. Take care of your physical, emotional, and mental well-being just like you care for your spiritual being. Get the proper amount of nutrition, rest, recreation, relaxation, fellowship, prayer, and Bible study.
12. You matter to God. He loves you and has good plans for your life. ".... plans to give you a hope and a future" (Jeremiah 29:11).
13. Females, remember men do not usually show off or reveal skin in their everyday dress. Their bodies are fully covered. As a young woman and as age takes over, please dress with dignity and discretion. It is good to dress modestly. This

means, covering your breast…they don't have to hang out or be seen. Keep your leg inside of your clothes instead of sticking your thigh out of a slit or wearing shorts so tight and high cut that genitals are seen. Lastly, don't' take photos with your legs spread apart from east to west as an open bridge. I interviewed a young intelligent gentleman to get his opinion about young women wearing "butt shorts." His reply: "I don't look at them. I considered that 'no class.' They'll be pregnant the next time I see them. That's all that's good for." I continued to probe. I asked what about the dresses with the high thigh splits? He said, "Well, some are classy, depending how they look." So, I asked, if you were married and you had a teenage daughter, would you want her to wear a dress with a high thigh split? It took him two to three minutes of meditation and he finally said, "No!"

14. What is your reasoning? Your outfit does not have to reveal every indent in your body. Spandex dresses? Why? Crossing your legs with a short skirt for your upper thigh to show? Why? Who do you want to see your upper thigh?! Who do you want to see your restricted areas in public? Do you think that you will attract a husband looking like a walking advertisement for sex? Are you a 'thirsty'/wanton woman? Modesty still works. You can still be drop-dead gorgeous without being drop-dead tacky or looking like a "thot," a teen

high school term I've heard former students use) or someone 'on a stroll!' (Check with the younger generation or use Google for the definition of 'thot')

15. Marriage is honorable! Participating in play a marriage set-up/shacking will not land you in the heavenly ports of eternity. Do not be deceived by deceptive terms of the day such as: "wifey," "fiancee' or "my only." If you're not legally married, you are still single, without financial or insurance benefits, as you would have if married. The Courts will not recognize you as a wife or husband if all you are doing is shacking!
16. Should God allow you to have children, you will be their example in all things, speech, mannerism, morals, dress, economical values, etc. Ask God to show you what is important and how to train your children in godly ways. Do not allow your children (nor yourselves) to adapt clothing styles to current revealing and criminal standards!. For males this means, not dressing or training your two-year-old toddler to look and dress like a 'gangsta rapper' with his oversized pants sagging, oversized shirt hanging, fake or real oversized gold chain necklace, cap backwards, etc. What are you raising? A drug dealer or a man of God with godly character? An intelligent princess with godly values and morals or someone who looks and behaves like a woman of the night or a thot. Your job is to train a child in

the way he should go, not the way the world and Satan would have them go. This will keep them safe from places and people who might do them harm and derail their godly purpose.

17. When you reach senior status, your adult children will express their own choices which may not agree with what you taught them. Do not stress. They are adults. Make sure you taught them the way they should go! Continue to pray and enjoy your peace.
18. Ask someone older who has godly wisdom for advice when you need it especially about insurances (medical, home, renters, car, life, etc.) This is important. Adulting is serious business.
19. Allow godly older family members or older close godly friends to meet the person you believe you are interested in as your future spouse. Allow that friend to have casual conversations with them and get private feedback. Just the two of you. Prayerfully receive their advice and proceed as God directs.
20. When you continue to experience the failures of the same nature, please seek godly wisdom. Remember, you are the only constant in each of these same experiences.

Remember, older people have lived long enough to see many blessings as well as afflictions throughout life. In every case, most survived their setbacks. Sometimes the survival methods God used for individuals changed the entire landscape of that individual's life. These changes may have included changes in living locations, careers, elimination of unhealthy emotional relationships, and parasitic attachments. These changes affect older people and younger people alike. Never feel insufficient, belittled, or resentful because an older person might empathize with your struggle and want to help. Receiving advice from someone older does not mean you are weak or unable to make the right decisions. It also does not mean you are a wimp or too. It does mean you are wise enough to know you do not know everything and might need a little advice sometimes. Older people can be an encouragement on your walk as a believer.

## RACISM- Views From Older Black Folks

"Even to your old age, I am He, And even to gray hairs, I will carry you. I have made, and I will bear: Even I will carry, and I will deliver you" (Isaiah 46:4, NKJV).

"You shall stand up before the gray head and honor the face of an old man, and you shall fear your God: I am the Lord" (Leviticus 19:32, ESV).

Why do black Folks gauge most things in their lives as either racist or not racist? We, older blacks have seen a lot over our lifetime. Discussion in this section present scenarios that black people have seen, heard about, or been through themselves that color their thinking. Some would say, "We've seen it all," but that would not be true. However, what we have seen can fill many books. Have you ever observed how some older folks walk or drive?

Have you observed how we as older folks watch and say nothing? We are weighing what we see against what we think should be happening from the viewpoint of our historical life's experiences. If you are under 60, you may not have given thought about aging. Is aging for a black person different that other ethnicities? If you have not given thought to what it will be like when you become older, you need to do a little research to prepare yourself. One of the profound experiences of life is aging. It happens slowly.

Some adults in their late thirties and early forties believe they have all knowledge and completely overlook life experiences of older people as a helpful resource. Many of these younger ones, if in their power and authority, place older folks on the shelf. This happens regardless of race. Others however remember and respect the advice and presence of their dearly beloved grandparents, great-aunties, and great-uncles, as well as other godly, kind, well-meaning elders. These experiences can vary. I must admit though, by the time this phase of life is reached for most blacks , the severe memory of life's joys, trials, racism, by other races are generally set. What should older black folks do? Many people avoid situations and people who may instigate some form of racial or age-related disrespectful experience. They may also pretend the situation does not exist and just suck it up. In other words, they wise up, avoid, and enjoy their lives. Period. They remember the queues of life that brought them to that point and have vowed to themselves and God they will not let it happen again.

Derogatory racist words will be inferred and not used in the text. Racist scenarios, statements, institutional activities are presented from a black perspective with the hope and prayers for understanding and change from white people. I am not saying that black people have reached perfection. Situations and scenarios are factual with names and places changed.

Many people believe whites do not understand that some of their behaviors are viewed blacks and others as racist. One likely reason for the lack of understanding is acceptance of their own behaviors as correct or a part of white privilege. Dialogue is needed between black and white Christian brethren if change and a love walk is to be achieved in the Body of Christ Jesus.

What are examples of racist behaviors that brought these older black to their conclusions of avoidance? Here is an example of an older Black man, Chad, who served his church for 40 plus years. Now in his seventies he was dismissed by the church's white, younger generation leaders. Chad was competent, astute, full of vigor and integrity to do whatever he was. One evening he served at a large event as an usher. His assignment was to keep seats reserved for pastors and their spouses by allowing two seats per couple. One white pastor refused to abide by the request after being politely asked twice. Chad continued his duties by seating others and doing the best he could to reserve pastoral seats. Then suddenly everything came to a halt. Chad had heard and seen many things during his pilgrimage while serving God at his church. Some of them he dismissed as foolishness but this time he had experienced for himself a hurtful life episode. He was called aside from his duties and summoned for a conference by two younger white ministers.

They took him to a private room and told him he needed to move to the back in a corner of the church if he wanted to serve. They said he was not the face the church wanted new people to see. Chad had served faithfully in practically every area of ministry and was taken aback, perplexed, and hurt.

He asked, "What wrong have I done?"

He was told nothing, but he needed to move. What should he have done? What could he do? What would you have done? As the story continued, he prayed and did not stay for the remainder of the service. He left and went home. During this age of technology, Chad had the presence of mind to video/audio record the encounter on his cell phone and he keeps it until this day. Did he ever report this? He made two attempts. One was successful to a sister in Christ and the other was unsuccessfully sent to a pastor. Chad prayed about it and let it go. He continued his fellowship with that church and struggled to forgive instantly the three younger white ministers for their disrespect. Chad eventually, quietly took a rest from the ministry. Chad wanted to enjoy the rest of his time on earth, loving and enjoying people who would love him as well. Chad experienced this disrespect and racism from the younger ministers and left the situation in God's hands. The bottom-line question is, why is this never discussed in a sermon with scriptural backup? There are other examples many shared but this will suffice for now.

"And even to your old age I am he; and even to hoar hairs will I carry you: I have made, and I will bear: even I will carry, and will deliver you" (Isaiah 46:4, KJV).

God said He will carry and sustain the aged. How will the younger future generations treat the aged in family, career, social, and church settings? Will they mimic what they see as young children? Someone intrinsically passed along racism. Aging is a daily process which can bring with your day of retirement, aches, pains, health concerns, increased doctors' appointments, and the possibility of downsizing. Many things in life affect people of any color. Guarding your heart, keeping joy, and health become extremely important as you age. Older blacks carry some limitations from over hundreds of years of unfair housing and lending policies designed to hinder their upward mobility. Society must still work to improve the Black life experience of aging. Housing for aging older Black folks still lags because of generational limited financial resources, which affects affordability. At least there are now some decent retirement facilities available.

Disrespect of the aged by younger folks did not fare well in one biblical story. A group of young men treated an older Prophet in the Old Testament disrespectfully. Many theologians say these young men were between the ages of 18-30 years old. There were 70 of these younger men. As the story goes, Elisha the prophet is on his way to Bethel after having caught the mantel of Elijah after the Spirit of God took him in a chariot of fire (2 Kings 2:11-15).

"Then he (Elisha} went up from there to Bethel; and as he was going up by the way, young lads came out from the city and mocked him and said to him, "Go up, you baldhead; go up, you baldhead!' 'When he looked behind him and saw them, he cursed them in the name of the LORD. Then two female bears came out of the woods and tore up forty-two lads" (2 Kings 2:23, NASB).

What an awful way for 42 young men to die because of their disrespectful and bullying antics to the old prophet! God left the other 28 alive to tell everybody about the entire ordeal. Perhaps younger men who learned about the terrible slaughter changed their minds about harassing an older prophet for fear of their lives. It appears no one taught these young men how to respect elders. Today we see non-black and non-brown men murdering black folks in church prayer meetings, grocery stores, and other places. Law enforcement arrests white murderers without physical violence or incident and even bring them Burger King for dinner. Selling cigarettes on the corner is probably illegal, but not deserving of death. The white man invited himself to the church prayer meeting, killed nine of the prayer warriors and was treated to a special meal by law enforcement officers, which is horrendous! Why was the murderer deserving of a lunch or dinner treat from Burger King?

This is what we see in American culture in the 21st century. Someone would have to be slow of mind to not see racism in these activities. Black Folks also see and weigh the actions of the church and did not see or hear very much. Where are the sermons about unjust and racist treatments in national and local televised Sunday services? Not much is being preached or come as a correction from white national pulpits. One might wonder what would happen if pastors taught them to respect older Blacks from pulpits? What would happen if God would allow an Elisha experience? Whatever the reason might have been, the bullying and disrespect did not work out for those young men who disrespected Elisha. Forty-two of them died. What can you say? It pays to respect your elders. Besides, Elisha was walking and minding his own business, not bothering a soul, and this happened to him. Clearly, the younger men never gave it a thought that Elisha might have had power from God or a special anointing to speak an active curse.

Racist behaviors and bullying are closely linked. Some non-Black folks have been committing violent and bullying behaviors towards blacks since the inception of the country, while most times it afforded them the continuance and lack of just penalty most times. There seems to be improvement through legal settlements and a few prison incarcerations for deathly and unjust treatment of innocent Black folks. Unlawful and violent treatment today is being labeled as "mental illness conditions" rather than lack of godly home training and/ white privilege. The lack of corrective sermons dealing with "the love walks" as they relates to race relations, Christian love, and racism, continues. Many times, white brethren are not open to discussions or addressing the issues in sermons because many want to continue pretending everything is fine.

Some white ministers preach "taking the country by force" to accommodate their political preferences, paired with gain and leadership dominance. Such pulpit leaders misuse Matthew 11:12 as a green light to take part in insurrections against the American government. The verse says: "from the days of John the Baptist until now the kingdom of heaven suffereth violence, and the violent take it by force" (KJV). Had Jesus wanted to take the kingdom of God by violence against the Roman government, He could have without human help. Black on Black violence is not being overlooked, but for this writing I am addressing racism as it appears to be inflicted on blacks. All non-whites observe the treatment of Brown-skinned folks from south of the border by White folks. Because of the terrible comments and political upheavals about their migration, they are now being labeled by many as the new blacks. That's putting it nicely by not using the racial slur.

**Prayer Point:**

*Lord Jesus, there are many things in life that are onetime experiences. Aging and becoming an older adult are a part of those experiences. Help us as we age to be more discerning of places and people who love us and those who have no need for us, as well as those who do. Help us to be pleased with your affirmation alone, not offended and do what is right in your sight and become content with your approval alone. Lord Jesus, please strengthen our minds, our bodies, and spirits to serve You wherever You lead and give us favor with younger folks. Allow us to so we can impart godly wisdom from the years You've given us to those who are younger that you send to us. May we find contentment and loving fellowship with those You send in our live Jesus's name. Amen.*

"Praise the LORD. Blessed is the man who fears the LORD, who greatly delights in his commandments. 2 His offspring will be mighty in the land; the generation of the upright will be blessed" (Psalm 112:1, ESV).

"Remember the days of old; consider the years of many generations; ask your father, and he will show you, your elders, and they will tell you" (Deuteronomy 32:7, ESV).

"And hath made of one blood all nations of men for to dwell on all the face of the earth, and hath determined the times before appointed, and the bounds of their habitation" (Acts 17:26, KJV).

"For there is no respect of persons with God" (Romans 2:11, KJV).

People have differing perceptions and definitions of racism. Some think it is the cold obvious hatred, disrespect, ill will, dismissive, oppressive, and vulgar actions of some whites against blacks, browns, and a few reds and yellows. I watched a recent interview with a white man discussing his desires to contribute a few dollars to send all black people in America back to Africa. He further stated how glad he was he was white. Here's a man you do not have to wonder if he is racist. He is!

Many blacks generally understand or define racism as deliberate, hateful, disrespectful, dismissive, ostracizing, and many times violent and murderous and other obvious evil actions. Most times, it is defined as something whites do against blacks. Those same whites never or hardly ever do those kinds of evils and schemes to their own. This includes from the lowest socio-economic level to the highest levels.

Many blacks, through the years have created their own definitions of racism by watching, listening, receiving the butt end of demeaning and dismissive jokes and discussions, manipulative closed economic and social doors, crookedness, and vulgar statements. The judgement of racist treatment is almost innate. One might say they are born with it in the same manner that they believe many whites have an innate racist lifestyle.

Many have passed down the belief of White racism/supremacy through the generations. They can demonstrate it, live it, and transfer without being verbally taught. No other ethnic group has received the butt end of white racism/supremacy In America, Native Americans, and brown people from the south of the border have often seen this treatment as well. The government put Native Americans away on reservations and told them to "stay!" They still struggle to gain state and national recognition while staying put on small fractions of the land that originally belonged to their ancestors. Why? A majority white Congress will not vote to change their recognition status. When Native Americans approach their state Legislature, they are told to make Congress do it.

I present a little expose from an article that explains additional areas of racism below. After this presentation, I will list examples of racist treatment and scenarios for your discussion, repentance, and new agape relationships with your non-white brothers and sisters. I believe a small percentage of whites do not realize when they are practicing a behavior that is racist, while the larger percent know but don't really give a care. It is my prayer that the stench, mental philosophy, and lifestyle of white supremacy and racism would fold up and die in Jesus' name.

The article on the next page further expounds on what needs to be understood.

"First, I have lost patience continuously explaining what it means to be privileged to a white person and why black pain is valid. Second, I understand that black people have a right to voice out their pain. Their pain does not require validation from a white person to be considered real. If your arrogance as a white person is blinding you from seeing this, then it is time you did some introspection. Do not be quick to jump on the "victim" bandwagon and accuse blacks of being racist. Black people can never be racist–we never had the tools or power to institutionalize racial oppression. So next time you as a white person want to accuse black people of reverse racism and insufficient anger–check yourself and your privilege.

May we learn to stop equating the need to speak out against racial inequality with "angry blacks" or "black people punishing whites." We do not have the time or energy or interest to hate – but what we do have time for is the emancipation of the black person both physically and mentally. Do not attempt to silence our voices. You will fail horribly at that. Black pain is valid, and it demands to be felt." —Sonant Mzwakali, October 13, 2015

I wrote this book during a time when advanced technology permits most people of all economic stations and ethnicities to own at least one portable electronic device. Access and ownership enable individuals to produce live recordings that can be transmitted and made visible all over the world while at the same time receive information via text, photos, phone, videos, and live feeds from any place on the planet. These devices were readily available when racial tensions erupted again in the United States of America. This tension shown worldwide on May 25, 2020, was because of brutal force by some white police officers against a black man and witnessed by the entire globe. These officers had no regard for black life nor integrity of the office they held. This lack of respect and lack of justice by white police officers was visible all over the world. Following that incident, significant worldwide racist murders and other events occurred for three to four continuous years.

One year prior, during January 2019, the discovery of the first case of COVID-19 occurred in America. COVID eventually became a worldwide viral pandemic. This virus mutated into many variants with one more deadly than others that wreaked havoc around the world. As of this writing, several pharmaceutical companies have developed vaccines to help prevent the devastating effects of COVID, yet 6.3 million people died worldwide from COVID-19. The chronological sequence of events during the pandemic in America was something like this:

1. The global pandemic- COVID-19 arrived.
2. Economic and social shutdowns due to COVID quarantines.
3. Mass murder of 10 blacks shopping for groceries by a white man on May 14, 2022). He is arrested

and taken alive. Prior to this atrocity, on June 17, 2015, a White mass murderer killed nine Black people at the Emanuel African Methodist Episcopal Church in Charleston, SC while thy attended a prayer meeting… which these loving Black folks had invited the mass murderer in to take part.

4. Increased injuries and deaths from black-on-black gun violence in their communities and many believe underground White racists provided the weapons.
5. Because of racial injustices through police brutality against black Americans, worldwide protest erupted and supported correction and require a change of racist, unjust murders, and other injustices against blacks.
6. Some church congregations took the side of white supremacy by verbalizing political language that supported racial tensions.
7. A new move surfaced around 2021 to include the History of Black American culture in US History curriculums throughout public schools in America. The movement is called CRT or Critical Race Theory. When that movement happened, many white Americans vehemently disapproved. Blacks immediately defined the disapproval as another way for whites to hide their evil treatment of blacks and secure their white supremacy status.

You might wonder why list these events? I listed them because blacks form many perceptions and views as they see, read, and hear of the reaction of some predominately white churches. We deem many of these reactions as white privilege.. For example, most blacks know of many black men being arrested and being nearly tortured to death. We look at how white males are arrested and placed in solitary confinement for protection after committing mass murder against blacks. Many white churches grew silent when these injustices occurred while proclaiming CDC mask wearing remediations to prevent COVID-19 showed a lack of faith. I have not heard too much rebuking and correction from white pulpits, yet we want trust and love to abide. The following events are post-Jim Crow. Jim Crow laws were state and local laws introduced in the Southern United States in the late 19th and early 20th centuries that enforced racial segregation. This makes b lacks folks wonder... will some of these people ever stop their hate, arrogance, bigotry, and their desire to be supreme? Now a review of some plausible scenarios.

1. Blatant vulgar public displays—Pickup trucks with Caucasian drivers displaying truck and car bumper stickers that use the lowest character vulgar words describing black females, including the first Asian/African American female Vice President of the United States of America. I'm almost sure that the individual driving that truck has never met and knows nothing about the character or personal lifestyle practices of the

black women he insults with his public bumper stickers. I wonder, *does he have a pastor?* I used to tell my students the only woman you know well enough to talk about is your mother!

2. Some whites are employing unfair hiring policies to employ others who look like them. They overlooked the black candidate's qualifications, education, experience, and tenure and hired the white candidate instead. That is discrimination and racism. Of course, in 1964, the United States of America passed an Equal Employment Opportunity law, as part of the Civil Rights Act, which worked sometimes. This law was to eliminate preferential treatments of whites over blacks; hiring, promotions, pay, etc., when the white person was less qualified. Illegal hiring and work manipulations, which included higher pay scale for whites and less for blacks for the same job responsibilities, prevailed. Sadly, these practices still thrive, but thankfully they are not as prevalent, although many people are attempting to revert to the old days. These discrepancies take evil underhanded planning to execute.
3. Terrorist racist tactics—Increased occurrences of "White Power" slang and signs on some public school walls while many well-known national white preachers support white extremist violence. They declare anyone who does not believe the way they do is hell bound and not saved! Upticks of the racial slur 'N' word by white students

(starting at the kindergarten age) bullying black students on secondary campuses, simultaneously threatening to lynch black students and nooses on campuses boost white power or supremacy. Someone noted these terrorist racist tactics increased between 2016-2020. Many will read this and say, "Well, blacks fluently use the 'N' word in their entertainment arenas." Many older blacks do not approve of its use, while others use the term to enhance their style in music, etc. Many of these entertainers fleece money from blacks that literally buy into excessive and vulgar use of the term. Some Blacks also consider the 'N' word an exclusive term of endearment" among themselves only. That means everybody cannot use it. Why? When non-blacks use it, they revisit the origins of pre-civil war enslavement and terminology. This comes from American History that is not included in History textbooks and not taught in schools.

4. Unequal housing opportunities. A Black family who hired a Caucasian realtor to assist them in finding a home was told by their realtor, "I'm not going to show you a home out there, those people (referencing whites) paid good money for their homes." Meaning; you cannot live in that subdivision because you are black. This is called redlining. The family did, however, purchase the property in the area while simultaneously threatening to fire the white realtor.

5. The Black family who had gone out for breakfast at a national chain restaurant one Saturday morning was discriminated against and derogatorily treated by their Caucasian waitress. They waited and watched several Caucasian customers arrive and had their orders taken and delivered to them by the white waitress. An inquiry was made of the waitress from the mother about the service and orders, and the waitress said, "Oh, okay." Then, as she left their booth, while the children watched and listened, the waitress went over to a Caucasian table and said out loud, "I got to go serve the 'D#@%n N#$@$rs.'" Complaints were filed with the restaurant's headquarters. This Restaurant chain eventually received racial discriminatory lawsuits from across the nation. All members of that black family received individual monetary settlements from the large restaurant chain for the racial discrimination they suffered through profane language and treatment. They paid monetary settlements across the nation! Although this happened years ago, these types of events still happen in 2022.
6. Ignorant church racist treatment. Depending on the church, some blacks practice tolerance in multicultural congregations while attempting to worship amid having to tolerate ungodly, vulgar, and demeaning comments about the first black President of the United States of America by Caucasian Christians. These derogatory remarks

flourished on social media and national Christian television networks. A black Christian related an experience with a Caucasian male while at church. He made comments about gender assignment not being correct for the first Black leaders of the free world and other inappropriate suggestive comments while in church. A Black woman in the service overheard the comment and asked the man, "Are you Mrs. O's gynecologist?" Here is the point. The audacity and arrogance to say and think out loud and not think it would bother a Black person is unconscionable! When this happens in a church on a Sunday morning, one wonders what happens daily in society?

7. Supremacist Treatment. While receiving service at a Public National Non-Profit Organization, a volunteer white woman with the organization began to yell loudly and point her finger at a senior aged black woman. The Black woman pointed her finger back and told her to "wait a minute...1865 and slavery has ended. You will not point your finger at me like that!" Older blacks are weary and will not allow this kind of treatment any longer!
8. Separatist photo depictions. Organizational ads can sometime present a racist bottom line by the exclusion of people, or the dominant presence of one race. If a variety of ethnic groups are present in the ad, the ad is perceived and received as being fair and non-racist. Many will read this

and say, "Black folks need to get over it!" Many Blacks would say that they are working on getting over it by not supporting businesses that have segregationist ads.

9. Blatant Lack Of Respect. Lack of respectful recognition is another form of marginalization from some whites. This behavior of disrespect manifests itself when a black person is put down or unrecognized for achievements, titles, etc. At the same time, white counterparts are recognized in the same areas of expertise blacks are overlooked. Examples would include and are not limited to appropriate use of surnames, professional titles, and proclaiming abilities of Caucasians and not blacks. Or using the old plantation scheme by choosing one black' to elevate to represent them all. Of course, this can create a environment of jealousy among the omitted which eliminates the love walk as directed in 1 Corinthians 13. Many would argue that the world is more casual today and/ we all go by first names now. Seriously? Try that with someone in ministry leadership! Call them by their first name and you would be in rebellion! You'd better say Pastor, Prophet, Evangelist, or Bishop, First Lady, Lady Elect, etc.! Many others would ask, "Who gave you permission to be so casual with me or address me in such a familiar way when I have seen you offer a different level of respect to white people?" Here is what some people need to learn

more about blacks and our culture. We respect our elders by honoring them with appropriate titles. This may all seem trivial to you. It is not to us. The expectation from some whites is for backs to be okay with the type of treatment they dish out. This reasoning is more evidence of the white privilege mentality. This stuff gets old and can become redundant.

10. Blacks have learned to survive. I have learned to live, enjoy life, and the blessings and trials God has allowed regardless of experienced racism. Does that mean I do not mind racism? No, it does not. It does mean that God's grace and mercy prevails in my heart and mind and helps me to get through the ugliness of racism. Those who perpetrate these actions and refuse to change or repent. Like the younger generation says, "That's on them and between them and their God." God has blessed me to have a few authentic Caucasian friends and acquaintances who are not racist, and I do appreciate and love them dearly. I thank God for their lives in a world that may not support their relationship with blacks. Social settings can become mean and disingenuous due to some people being oblivious to their white privilege status. Customs from past generations filters down from generations of accepted racist behaviors are veiled to the point that it is almost unbreakable. Many are not disingenuous, and others have changed their ways. God can and does make "all

things work together for our good. God makes all things work together for good to those that love Him and are called according to His purposes." Romans 8:28.

11. Black analysis—Some blacks determine that many white people who perpetuate racist behaviors will not be in their close zone. While others will continue the way they are and not examine themselves or always see themselves as right. This is how some black folks see white privilege working out as "I'm right because I'm white." Some whites who say they have no racist problems, never publicly address the situation, or apologize for wrong behaviors. They just move along with life. For those people, you need to know that people remember your lack of response when opportunities were available and you didn't respond. This is especially true when you are provided a public platform to do so.

There is no wonder that the great divide among the races still exits. Much prayer, repentance, and change are needed for God's love to become genuine among His children. Jesus dealt with racism in His pilgrimage on earth. The Jews had nothing to do with the Samaritans. You might say the Samaritans were treated like today's black, brown, or red people and the Jews would represent some of whites. Why? Jews of the first century wanted their race to remain pure but some of the Jews intermarried with the Samaritans which led to children. They were looked down on by the Jews as an impure race. Jesus steps on the scene and let His disciples know that Samaritans were rightful heirs to the kingdom of God like Jews and Gentiles. The Apostle Paul declares that the only exception to a marriage partner besides being not being of the opposite sex (Romans 1:26-29) is that they believe in Jesus Christ as Lord and Savior. He says, "marry only in the Lord." In other words, marrying a Christian or believer in Christ is the only prerequisite (1 Corinthians 7:39-40). If a minister or pastor cannot say or affirm this, there might be a little heart cleaning issue. Only God knows the heart.

Views of racism were discussed by God's servant, the late Evangelist Billy Graham, in an article written by Mike Ruffin. The article, "But he needed to go through Samaria," *was* based on John 4:4.

> "I wrote this column over 10 years ago. Obviously, tragic events across the country once again show that we are nowhere close to overcoming racism. In fact, it is probably worse today than it has been for years.
>
> Billy Graham has said for years that the greatest problem facing America is racism. In fact, Graham's book *A Prophet with Honor* recalls that in 1953 Graham "dismissed as unbiblical the racist contention that dark skin and the inferior social standing of blacks (were) derived from a curse Noah placed on Canaan, the son of Ham (Genesis 9.22-27), and were therefore a part of a divinely sanctioned and unchangeable order. To the question: Does

the Bible teach the superiority of any one race, he replied: 'Definitely not. The Bible teaches that God hath made of one blood all the nations of the world ... Anthropologists have come to two important biological conclusions. First, there are no pure races; and there are no superior or inferior races.'"

In *Peace with God*, Graham lamented, "When true Christians look at other people, they see no color, nor class, nor condition, but simply human beings with the same longings, needs and aspirations as our own."

Don't you find it unusual that we rarely hear a sermon on racism? Why? And what does the Bible really have to say about the practice of racism?

Frankly, I think most pastors in today's churches shun the subject of racism because it is not good for numbers. The fact is if they make their members uncomfortable, they may go to another church in search of comfort. Since declining membership can spell financial trouble, they avoid the sermons that their members may find objectionable. Hopefully, the next few weeks will prove me wrong." *

How sad it is that even today, racism still plagues the Christian church, and many pastors are afraid to address the issue in depth. Why? Fears of losing funding from certain parishioners, fear of not being fully persuaded to identify racist issues existing among parishioners, and God forbid, even in their own hearts. The amount of personal conflict experienced by many blacks as they journey to serve God is expressed in a few statements by W.E.B. DuBois in his book, *Souls of Black Folk.*

1. "One ever feels his twoness, —an American, a Negro; two souls, two thoughts, two unreconciled strivings; two warring ideals in one dark body."
2. "Either America will destroy ignorance or ignorance will destroy the United States."
3. "The Nation has not yet found peace from its sins; the freedman has not yet found in freedom his promised land."

Since 2022 talk across America about instigating a new Civil War. White people have become so dissatisfied they are willing to destroy the entire country for their privilege. W.E.B. DuBois and many other notable scholars have prophesied the internal destruction of America. We will either learn to live as God says by loving one another or suffer the consequences of not having an America as we know it today. Therefore, what do we do? We keep praying, hoping, living for God, and doing the best we can in order to live a life for God. That will allow us to have joy as we walk in a world filled with hate for folks that look like us. We avoid the heart-rending questions: Will this ever change? Do we have to continue to make laws to receive fair treatment while we know years later lawmakers will systematically overturn these laws as they do in voting issues? Are these people so filled with arrogance that they seriously believe they are better than everyone else on the planet?

**Prayer Point:**

*Heavenly Father, thank You for the opportunity to ask for Your mercy and grace to be poured out on our hearts that we can have the abundance of mercy and love to forgive mistreatment by many who demean us. We pray that the revelation of Your Word that says all humanity was created from one blood become alive in the hearts of all men regardless of color. While we pray for our situation, we do not forget others, but right now we are asking for help for all races. We ask for healing of wounds, riddance of racism, humility for those who are privileged to repent and humbly change and finally complete unity and love among us all. Your church and Your Name must be glorified and we indeed would become one. We ask your favor for those of other ethnicities who spend their lives helping to make things right for everyone else. Bless them abundantly. Let us all examine ourselves, repent, and love each other as you intended. In Jesus' name, Amen.*

**References:**

(All Scripture references from the Public Domain of various translations)

1. *Alexandria Proffet,- (Former Student, Baton Rouge, Louisiana, 2021)*
2. https://biblehub.com/commentaries/expositors/genesis/1.html
3. *Christian Broadcasting Network (CBN) 1-800-700-7000*
4. Ishmael: Ishmael – Wikipedia en.wikipedia.org › wiki ›, 2020
5. *Kenneth Hagan Ministries (KHM) –1-918-258-1588 M-F 8:15am-4:30pm (CST)*
6. Racism Article -https://independenttribune.com/lifestyles/faith-and-values/column-what-the-bible-has-to-say-about-racism/article_78cacf78-a95b-597a-9b9c-c11939084fd4.html

# NOTES

# My Story of Three

### (Retirement, Cancer, and the Great Flood of 2016)

### Retirement – May 2016

Most life-changing events are usually unexpected. My Internal Revenue Service filing status is Head of Household. That means I am single and oversee all my financial responsibilities for tax purposes. I have had this status for thirty-three years and now I am ready to retire. Those thirty-three years include my children becoming adults, finishing college, and serving God and living independently on their own.

Thinking of retirement now, became easier. I observed people work about 25 to 30+ years during their lifetime aiming towards retirement, yet not visualizing nor planning for it. My prayer for years was to have the strength to raise my children and become debt free. I always hoped it would happen, but never knowing exactly how God would allow or make it happen. Therefore, I continued to pray about it and placed it down on the bottom of the manifestation list. Meanwhile I paid my tithes , managed my finances, saved, and spent frugally.

A heart-rending abrupt career end became a

miraculous "all things working together for my good" entry into a career that would open doors for me. I planned to be accepted as a new student in the Doctoral Program. This change would shortly add a terminal professional degree, which increased my salary and retirement benefits. God had already allowed me to earn a Master's Degree. Additional credentials and certifications were also blessings that came with the life-changing event of abandonment and divorce. Earning the Doctorate Degree helped to bring about my retirement security and liberty from inherited debt through divorce.

Through wisdom from God, I initiated God's divine purpose for my liberation from debt. The debt, inherited from marriage, from the dissolved marriage for keeping the home and mortgage transferred completely in my name. The mortgage and all other matrimonial debts were mine to manage and eliminate. I worked my full-time teaching job and part-time employment as an University Adjunct Instructor for two universities and a part-time home inspector for 10 years. God gave me wisdom and direction on how to put money aside to send my two children to college. I could receive scholarship monies for my own Doctoral graduate studies.

Many people who knew me never knew how hard I worked while raising my children. They never asked, and I never volunteered the information. I enrolled in Graduate School, got certified in two additional teaching areas, and worked a full-time and part-time jobs. God was faithful in providing strength and part-time jobs that allowed me to work from home or bring my children with me. As a matter of fact, many were surprised when they heard that I graduated with a doctorate because I did not discuss the process with many people. One sister in the Body of Christ and her husband were privy to my journey and when I graduated, they gave my family and I am wonderful graduation party in their home. When the time was right, God eliminated all part-time jobs, and my salary was enough to support us. Philippians 4:19 states, "And my God shall supply all your need according to His riches in glory by Christ Jesus" (NKJV). God has always been faithful.

Now here I am, at the ripe age of sixty-nine, and I prayerfully begin to execute my career exit plan and begin my retirement journey. Whether you are male or female, there will be a time, should God allow you to live long enough, that you will consider your retirement and how you will manage financially during those years. My professional career included various fields of Education: University Graduate School Adjunct Instructor Northwestern Louisiana State University, LSU Ag. Center Home Economist, LSU Distance Learning HS Instructor, School District Instructional Support Specialists, Public and Private Classroom Teacher, and Fellowship of Christian Students/Athletes (FCA) Volunteer.

The exact time and day of my departure was not plain but as you will see later, God has a way of making things noticeably clear. God desires to guide us by His Holy Spirit. He wants the best for us. He said through Jesus, "I'll never leave you nor forsake you" (Hebrews 13:5). Ask of me and I will show you great and mighty things" (Jeremiah

33:3). As we lean on Him through daily prayer, Bible study, and listening, we gain wisdom and understanding. God's timing is especially important; One important consideration for retirement was provision for my medical insurance. I knew that I qualified (due to age) for Medicare. I did not know my medical insurance payments would be affordable and would provide a plan for no out-of-pocket expenses for major medical treatments. I also didn't have co-payments for regular doctor visits, specialists, or assistance for medications. Praise God! His faithfulness kept coming and He never stopped. I continued to place God first by tithing, financially responsible planning, and believing God's promises about His provisions for me when I tithed.

Malachi 3:10-11 tells us, "Begin by being honest. Do honest people rob God? But you rob me day after day. "You ask, 'How have we robbed you?' "The tithe and the offering—that's how! And now you are under a curse—the whole lot of you—because you're robbing me. Bring your full tithe to the Temple treasury so there will be ample provisions in my Temple. Test me in this and see if I do not open heaven itself to you and pour out blessings beyond your wildest dreams. For my part, I will defend you against marauders, protect your wheat fields and vegetable gardens against plunderers." (MSG).

There were three areas of preparation I believe the Lord gave me to prepare for surviving three life-changing events. "If any of you lacks wisdom, let him ask God, who gives generously to all without reproach, and it will be given him" (James 1:5 ESV):

1. Listening in prayer to that still small voice that guided me in making financial decisions and purchases was key. Many of these impressions preceded the events and were implemented to assist the completion of these began many years before the coming events. These included varying but distinct insurance plans and participation in Louisiana Deferred Retirement Option Plan (DROP*) as soon as I was eligible. This plan offered by Louisiana Teacher's Retirement System allowed me to not pay into retirement for three years and the monthly amount that would have been subtracted from my monthly salary was now added into my take-home salary. DROP also was a savings plan that automatically saved each month for 36 months the projected monthly pension check that I would receive if I were actively retired! That is 36 times my projected monthly retirement check! That provided a nice savings account when I retired. Praise God!
2. I began to save and reduce debt with the increase in my salary check due to the DROP three-year enrollment and increase in salary. The increase was due to step level increase in pay after earning a Doctorate degree
3. I budgeted (the budget also included monies set aside for monthly payments for a cash cancer policy and savings for my yearly FEMA flood insurance policy) and debt reduction plan in place

when the DROP was complete when leaving the workforce. In other words, how to use my current monthly salary and projected savings from my DROP account so my monthly retirement budget would be manageable for my expenses. It was still my prayer and desire to become debt free!

I believe all the planning would not have been successful if God had not given me wisdom, His grace, and mercy to honor Him in the tithe and offerings for 30 plus years. Tithing for me meant giving 10% of all my earnings before taxes to God via my local church affiliation and I placed 10% into savings as well. The 80% salary after tithe and savings covered my expenses with extra remaining. By then, in my sixty-ninth year on the planet, I give more than the tithe by supporting additional ministries and charitable organizations. The thought of retirement became achievable and concrete. Many ministries today teach tithing is unnecessary or even outdated because it is a part of "the Law." To them I say, God has proven Himself faithful to me in the process of tithing and you can well do what you like. I will stick with tithing.

"And thine ears shall hear a word behind thee, saying, This is the way, walk ye in it, when ye turn to the right hand, and when ye turn to the left" (Isaiah 30:21, KJV).

God is faithful in getting our attention when mapping out plans for our future. As I prayerfully sought direction from God, things began to happen. For me it started with the impression to retire soon. While having these impressions and praying about it, God used people who knew nothing of my prayers. These people, would unknowingly to them, confirm what I was praying about.

Here is one example of what happened one day while I was at work. "You really need to get your money out of retirement," said the seasoned speckled gray-haired union representative professional. "You never know what could happen."

I stared at him and pondered those words. I had been meditating on retirement for months. My three-year deferred retirement option plan (DROP) was complete. For each year I continued to work beyond the three-year DROP completion, my projected monthly pension check would increase in value. Retirement now seemed achievable. I kept believing to become debt-free (Romans 13:8. Owe nothing to anyone--except for your obligation to love one another). I still did not know exactly how that would come about except I reasoned it would take about twenty more years of strict management of my finances after retirement. That would make me eighty-nine years old! Reviewing my expenses, I determined I could retire my car note and only have one large bill—the mortgage—my tithe, and living expenses.

Retirement for me became increasingly achievable. I no longer had the responsibility of child rearing, assisting my children with their college tuitions and other expenses. God blessed me to pay those college fees for them "as- you-go" and after they graduated college. That Louisiana Teacher's Retirement DROP plan really came in handy. Sometimes, when God is preparing us for what lies ahead, we do not know what we are currently doing is for something in the future. The closed door from my previous employment ushered me into God's divine provision. I thank closed doors for being closed.

Over my lifetime, I became professionally consistent in saving every dime. Coupons, sales, extended use warranties, membership rewards with various banks and stores, legal savings, and any legal shortcut savings. Implementing these saving techniques were my daily mantra in utilizing finances (mine, yours, or anyone else's) God has allowed me to steward. By the way, it still is my way of life. I have managed funds for several organizations and their finances were always in the black with monies left over.

Getting life's necessities and extras as close to free or without expense is always a good thing. My rewards points allowed me to vacation free most times without hotel fees. Transportation was free as well when I saved up enough points to travel. God answered my prayers for wisdom in managing my finances. I accomplished this by using designated credit cards that gave points for specific use. Some of these cards even allowed points to be used for gifts card purchases from other merchants. I sometimes used those for Christmas gift cards. The key to using these designated credit cards is to charge only what you know you will pay off each month, such as utilities, tithes, and other monthly expenses. I was happy when I could use one of my favorite bank cards instead of a check for tithing. God allowed me to bring Him His portion, gain points and pay one credit card for the increase. Someone asked me, "Do you get points when you don't pay off your card each month?"

I said, "I don't know, I've never not paid them off each month to know what happens if you don't pay the entire balance."

I have been blessed to include monthly living expenses such as phone, all insurances, all utilities, tithes, and some extras in my budget and I pay them off monthly using bank cards that carry rewards points..

In the middle of May 2016, I began the official paperwork process to retire. I started with visiting the Louisiana State Teachers' Retirement Office to make sure all my ducks were in a row. I looked at the beneficiaries, distribution of my DROP account, financial institution for deposits and dates for to begin my disbursements. My final signatures were official on May 25, 2016. Praise God, I was officially retired. With the elated wonder feelings of retirement came the intrusion of a doctor's visit. It seemed to me a delayed diagnosis allowed by God. He had permitted me to work for over 40 years with no surgeries or weeks off from work because of illnesses. God allowed me to raise my children and put them through college before the trial of sickness came along. I am grateful for His divine timing. My mother left for heaven in 1991. For 25 plus years, God strengthened me to live in a city where my only blood relatives were my children. Thank you, Jesus.

## Cancer – May, July, and August 2016

"For I know the plans I have for you," says the LORD. "They are plans for good and not for disaster, to give you a future and a hope" (Jeremiah 29:11, NLT).

"For there is a proper time and procedure for every delight, though a man's trouble is heavy upon him" (Ecclesiastes 8:6, ASV)

In the middle of ending my career for retirement, the diagnosis came. It was breast cancer. God gave me strength, wisdom, and soundness of mind to plan, retire, attend a family out-of-state wedding, and return for surgeries. I really enjoyed an uplifting time with my family prior to surgery. The Holy Spirit helped me to guard my faith, mind, and activities with all diligence because this trial wanted to promote fear. God provided comfort and strength in the following three areas to walk through this trial:

1. Strength and courage to pray, hang on to, and confess the promises of God daily, live as normal as possible daily, and stay at peace. My loving daughter helped me tremendously. I lived with her for seven months during renovations of my flooded home, recovery from surgery, chemotherapy, and radiation treatments.

2. Courage to confide in those who I thought loved me and would pray for me during this trial. Wisdom and discernment regarding who to share with was important to me. Why? I did not believe everyone who smiled in my face cared for me. My life had too many betrayals and blindly trusting people was no longer an option for me. Through God's kindness and mercy, he sent three sets of Christian sisters to pray for me and encourage me from three different churches and each church had different denominational backgrounds! God is amazing. At this stage of life, I served in three different churches. There were a few precious souls who stood with me all the way. I thank God for their love, prayers, gifts, and concern.
3. God made His presence tangible during both chemotherapy and radiation treatments. During and after the first radiation treatments, my experience with God and His presence was beyond expression. I thank and I give Him all the honor, praise, and glory for the supernatural peace He provided.

Years prior, I did spiritual warfare, binding cancer in Jesus' name and praying healing Scriptures. I also received prayers of agreement for healing over my body for yearly mammograms. Since age 35, I faithfully had mammograms each year. I hated the word cancer and still hate it. I hated every fund-raising, march, and announcement about the sickness, but I supported research with monetary donations. My donations went to M.D. Anderson for cancer research. Why? Because my mom had cancer. Because I loved my mother and hated the disease! I felt the best I could do was support the research, but I could never wear that "pink ribbon." I never told people why I did not wear that ribbon. It was not their business. This may seem selfish, but that is how I felt. I always prayed for others who suffered from this sickness with compassion, while believing God each year for my own good reports after each mammogram. This is my testimony of God's faithfulness to me.

Twelve years earlier, before retirement, God impressed me to purchase a "first diagnosis" cancer insurance policy. I selected the affordable basic reimbursement amount of $10,000.00. My monthly payments were about $21.00 and automatically deducted from my checking account. That was all I could afford. I made the monthly premium payments even though I hoped I'd never need this policy! I paid this premium faithfully over the years. It was something God impressed me to do, and He gave me resources to take care of it, even with all the other large financial responsibilities. As I worshipped God daily, the responsibilities of work, motherhood, graduate school, serving at my local church, and only plain living remained. God was always faithful during those early days when my children were growing up. They never lacked the necessities of life. God's faithfulness brought me through every trial and heartache. My children would spend their summer vacations in Houston with my brother and his wife and sometimes with my mom. They were loving and generous with my children. That gave me a two-week break each summer.

I never wanted to use that cancer insurance claim form, even though I made the premium payments for twelve years. God knew my future and that lump sum payment from the claim would help eliminate expenses that brought me closer to becoming debt free during retirement. Praise God! His plans for us are good. It is particularly important to listen and follow those still small voice impressions. I did not want cancer, yet God impressed me to purchase the cancer policy. He knows in advance our life's path.

"Whatever the LORD pleases, he does, in the heaven and on the earth, in the seas and all their deeps" (Psalm 135:6, ESV).

Several days after an automobile accident where I had been broadsided, I noticed red bruising to my right breast due to the seat belt. I checked with my physicians to see if any other complications could be hidden behind this bruising and there was none. What a relief. My Lexus SUV was placed in the shop and repaired, and I continued to teach.

During that school year, I felt the impression that it was time for me to retire. I had 40 plus years of professional work under my belt. I had worked on the planning of my finances and was giving the idea or retirement great thought and prayer. Now, here is where it gets heavy. A year later, my right breast showed similar redness as in the bruising right after the accident. My most recent mammogram was clear. I had them yearly without fail. There were no lumps and no available discharges to see. I went in anyway to have it checked out. The diagnosis came a month later with cancer in my right breast. Numb is the word I felt. I felt no fear only numbness, but I was willing to follow the medical professionals' advice. My daily prayer life and quiet time with God never changed. This included the reading of God's Word, worship in song in my spirit or aloud, keeping a daily journal of what God speaks to me each day. Finally, I wrote down my daily prayer request and new requests according to what He spoke to me that day. Now my prayer time included healing confessions that were more than the normal confessions of my daily routine.

I stood in the mirror and talked to the Lord. I said, "Lord, knock this weight off and get me that $10,000." That was a funny joke to me. Something between the Lord and me. Still, deep brooding and fearful meditations to the diagnosis I received attempted to impede my peace but did not. I spent most of my mental time planning my retirement logistics. Deciding which monthly expense to eliminate or reduce was important. My pension would be lower than my normal monthly salary; one of the larger payments needed to be eliminated, either the car or mortgage payment. My aim in prayer was to become debt free.

For many years I walked around my property lines and confessed that every place my foot shall tread, I shall possess (Joshua 1:3). God was listening. Little did I know a whole lot of water would be coming my way soon. I was completing the retirement paperwork to becoming medically insured as a retiree. I didn't know how all things were working together for my good (Romans 8:28). Still numb while robotically going to lots of doctors' appointments and being told what to do by my physicians, I continued with my daily activities. That included the Baton Rouge Symphony Chorus Rehearsals, Fellowship of Christian Students/Athletes, football ministry meetings, serving at the church where I fellowshipped. A surprise came later.

God had gave me two angels, one son, Andy, and one daughter, Dorcas. My son lived in another state and my daughter lived in her own home in the city where I lived. My angel in residence was my daughter. I prayed and asking God what to name her before she was born. God gave me a dream, and I knew she would be a little girl. I did not have a gender reveal (they were not popular during that time), I had a God reveal. All by Himself through the dreams, He gave me her gender and name, Dorcas. She is a female disciple (Acts 9:36) filled with good works. My daughter, Dorcas, was my faithful "go-to" person. She cared for me as I lived in her home, and it became my temporary residence for the next seven months when the next life changing survival trial came, The Great Flood of 2016 in the state of Louisiana.

Daily prayer time and worship became my greatest comfort. The presence of God sustained me through the numbness of these three simultaneous life-changing events. Chit chats with people? Not much. I really did not share or talk to people about my trials. Now and then I would provide specific health prayer requests to selected people. My confidants were my children, my brother, and his wife, and two saints in the church. God impressed me in prayer by asking, "what would you be doing if you did not have this diagnosis?" He then said, "Do it!" I lived as normally as possible. What God impressed me to do may not be God's plan for you, but this might help someone you know. Most times, God is individually specific in providing directions for His children. Each person who might go through this type of trial may have a different leading by the Holy Ghost.

You might wonder why I did not discuss this situation with others? For over 40 years of my Christian walk, I observed and listened to other believers' comments when they heard of someone's illness. I listened to questions asked of people who were ill, and it seemed to me that those questions were too personal. My mother raised me to never ask a person about their hospital stays or illnesses. Therefore, I obeyed her teachings and felt that the answers to the questions were confidential information and nobody else's business. I learned a lot from these observations and I did not want to be interrogated, harassed, or judged concerning why I might have this diagnosis. I had enough to go through without all the drama and small group "extra loud prayers" after church! Gee, if I wanted the entire church to know, I could have asked for a microphone.

Many people, even Christians seem to enjoy sprouting off what they think they know about someone, and they are not always correct. I do not know if you have ever been around a "know-it-all" and "know the cause" Christian;

but if you have, you'll learn to keep your mouth closed many times. I had enough to deal with and did not need to rehearse their perceptions in my mind. My mind had enough to fight without fighting the heard and unheard or imaginary unnecessary comments. I stood in faith for healing, surgeries, treatments, and couldn't believe the comments and questions some people gave me while at church? Hopefully, this illumination will help many people to understand and emphasize with others. Also, it is important to bridle our tongues. Individual personalities differ, and some personality types might not mind the interrogations. I do! Please ask God before you begin to ask questions. Jesus knows everyone's mind, heart, individual past, and sufferings. Your comments might do more harm than good.

Here are a few of the unnerving comments that resonate in the mind of a person going through the battle. If you already know this, maybe you can pass the information on to others to prevent interrogations and further injure the already afflicted:

"I hear that has something to do with unforgiveness. "

"What stage is it?"

"Wow, are you losing weight?"

"You know people will say, 'I wonder how long they've got?'"

"Did you lose your hair?"

"Is that your hair?"

"How many treatments do you have to have?"

"How long have you been in treatment?"

"Are you depressed?"

"Well, you're going to die with something."

As I said earlier, when I was a little girl, my mother taught me to never ask someone why they were in the hospital or what was wrong with them.

I said, "Yes, ma'am."

I can see why this is an effective way to live life. If someone is ill, let that person be the one to initiate the conversation concerning what their issue is. If someone wants you to know about their illness, they will let you know.

Quizzing is unacceptable to me. Through firsthand experiences, I have learned my mother was right! I admonish everyone to reign in their tongue when attempting to comfort or help a person going through any life-changing event. Do not become one of Job's friends. Job's friends accused him of many hurtful things. I suggest you read the book of Job in the Old Testament to understand how his friends were not much of an encouragement to him. Let Job and his friends become a lesson to remember when friends need encouragement.

"But no human being can tame the tongue. It is a restless evil, full of deadly poison" (James 3:8, ESV).

Attempting to be kind and loving to members of the Body of Christ can be challenging. People cross personal boundaries many times. Many believe that since you are Christian, they can ask you anything and expect you to answer no matter how personal.

"And He did not answer him with regard to even a single charge, so the governor was quite amazed" (Matthew 27:14 NASB).

Even Jesus did not answer questions all the time. This experience also made me think before I made a comment on someone's weight loss unless they are already discussing the issue. A few people do not realize that chemotherapy treatments can cause loss of appetite and weight loss. I did not experience vomiting and nausea, but loss of appetite happened to me following treatments. God knows I needed to lose the weight. I was slightly overweight. Being five feet, eight inches tall worked to hide my 40 pounds of "overweightness." After treatments, I lost 25 pounds. That was a good thing and I'm glad about it.

People would ask me, "How did you lost the weight?"

I would answer, "I eat smaller meals and climbed stairs up to my daughter's third floor vintage condominium that didn't have an elevator in the building." The answer was correct, but I did not mention chemo. It was none of their business.

I retired at the end of the school year, telling no one but my nearest family members about my upcoming surgery and retirement. Three of my pastors, one from each church, and selected intercessors, were privy to my condition. My co-workers did not know. Usually, the school provided a retirement recognition event for staff members. I did not feel up to it and except for my superiors, I did not share that I was retiring. I avoided all questions. Surgeries began in July during the same summer of my May 2016 retirement. You can tell I had trust issues. Trusting others became suspect to me because of past slights, rejections, and many betrayals. However, we know Romans 8:28 says all things work together for good. God had something in mind even during this situation. I used toll-free prayer lines to national ministries like Kenneth Hagan and CBN to help me with intercession for my condition.

One day, I was invited to a Cancer Survivors' luncheon. I sat next to a total stranger. A lady struck up a conversation while I sat next to her at the Cancer Celebration of Life event. The conversation centered on our various treatments. I mentioned to her I did not tell the entire church about my current state, only a few selected prayer intercessors.

She smiled and said, "I did the same thing. I only told three people in my church."

Wow, that gave me such comfort. Just think, God would allow me to sit next to a total stranger who had the same inclinations as I about sharing with others. It made me feel I was not alone. God is faithful to encourage us with what we need when we need it.

"The steps of a good man are ordered by the Lord: and he delighteth in his way" (Psalm 37:23, KJV).

The pastor of True Vine Baptist Church, a small but loving church, made sure I had two sisters from the church to sit with my daughter while I was in surgery receiving a lumpectomy. The surgery was a success, and they treated me as an outpatient, only to call me three days later after they discovered that several of my lymph nodes needed removal.. I thank the Lord often for the two sisters who came to sit with my daughter. Two other sisters came from the two other churches where God allowed me to serve. God did amazing things in showing His love for me, especially when He knew how much skepticism I have regarding trust. Two sisters came by from the Full Gospel church and visited with me before surgery. One of my female pastors from the First United Methodist Church came by while I was in surgery, and she visited with my daughter. During that season of my life, I went where every door was open where I could use the gifts God placed in me. I have been faithful in one home church, Bethany World Prayer Center for 39 plus years, and at the time of this event, I served two other churches as well. These two additional churches were different denominations and they both placed an emphasis on loving Christ and serving people.

Still, I lived my life on the last word I received from the Lord, "What would you be doing if you were not in this situation?"

I thought about it and the many activities I might do, and the still small voice said, "Do them."

That meant the first instructions were still valid in my life. Not only was God allowing me to give myself and gifts to others within the Body of Christ, but He gave me something to meditate besides what I was going through. This kept me spiritually, mentally, and physically strong. I would not recommend the schedule I had to someone else on any given Sunday, unless this was a confirmation of what God was leading them to do. If He leads you to it, He will provide the strength and what you need to finish. My schedule would consist of two and sometimes three Sunday morning services. One church I would serve as pulpit leader for the order of the services, and at another, I would serve in their folk choir and lay leader. Lastly, at another I would serve on their ministry team and Bible group leader.

There were times I could see the concern in my daughter's eyes and hear it in her voice. My first procedure occurred prior to the upcoming great flood of 2016. My daughter stayed with me for the first two nights after my first surgery and then I cared for myself. Having a drain bag attached to my body for lymph node drainage was something to get used to. The total of all surgeries, including biopsies, was four. Each procedure I had was as an outpatient, with one exception. I spent only one night in the hospital.

Continuing my daily activities included using a safety pin under my clothing to secure the drain pouch to keep the world from noticing the bag. It went everywhere with me. I must add, God gave me the strength and mental ability to do these things (drive, shopping, etc., independently). No one noticed or knew except my daughter and my physician.

Continuing life's activities kept my mind occupied and free from depression. God really knew what He was doing in speaking to my heart about continuing activities. The many activities I was involved in required driving to and from several weekly and biweekly evening rehearsals, scheduled group meetings, school volunteer club meetings, etc. I was a remarkably busy camper. Praise God for His mercy and open doors for ministry.

Eventually I felt the Lord prompting me to help others with encouraging words of faith with my experiences of diagnosis, surgeries, treatment, and the emotional ups and downs, fears, and "people." God knew I did not enjoy talking about cancer, but He opened doors for me to speak to others with a word of encouragement or offer a prayer. The Scripture promise is Revelations 12:11: "And they have defeated him by the blood of the Lamb and by their testimony. And they did not love their lives so much that they were afraid to die" (New Living Translation).

God provides instructions from His Word and will sometimes use people in different settings to lead and guide. He intends for us to use the Scriptures as a lifestyle. The main Scripture in this instance was, 1 Corinthians 1:3-4: "Blessed be the God and Father of our Lord Jesus Christ, the Father of mercies and God of all comfort, who comforts us in all our affliction so that we will be able to comfort those who are in any affliction with the comfort with which we ourselves are comforted by God."

My affliction was a diagnosis of breast cancer. The Lord brought me through this affliction, or trial as some call it, and I could help and encourage others in their walk of the scary and unknown. When God brings us through trials, we are to use the experiences He allowed to show and tell others of His unfailing love and mercy. This too revolves around God's timing. I had to come out of my shell first because I did not want to share anything with anybody. His mercy is great and new every morning.

The Holy Spirit's conviction continued to prompt me to come out of my shell of fear and distrust. I had to testify or share with others who needed comfort and encouragement about God's unfailing loving kindness to me. The question that lingered in my mind was, "How would I inform others outside of my small, designated circle I'd been through this ordeal?"

Not to worry. A fantastic opportunity arrived with an annual gala event called "Bust Breast Cancer Gala." This event was held at a large resort auditorium venue with local media coverage. They invited breast cancer survivors to attend, walk down a runway waving pink pom-poms, and cheer each other on. This is an annual fund-raising endeavor to support research and cancer patients. My daughter took a video of my stroll down the runway, and we posted it on my Facebook page. Facebook became a ministry platform/outlet for God to use my testimony of His faithfulness. Now, because of that FB video, my trial of cancer was no longer secret. That video allowed friends and acquaintances to know. God used that video and allowed me to connect with others who might need encouragement in their walk-through breast cancer. An abundance of comforting comments and reactions came from that post. Expressions ranged from how they did not know, to they were happy I made it through. Those comments were a great comfort and encouragement. After that experience, prayer requests increased, and I was joyful to help. Trials will and can bring the love of Christ and compassion to our hearts towards others experiencing the same or similar experiences.

Two years after treatment, the need in my heart to continue helping others and share my testimony increased. A former colleague underwent chemo treatments. She was advised by doctors to have radiation treatments as well. She was afraid and asked for information on a FB post.

Facebook can sometimes be a great thing for helping others. Some people condemn Facebook and other social media as all bad because they believe it decreases face-to-face social interactions and promotes other ills. That may be true in some cases, but not all of time. At the time of this writing, COVID-19 changed that perception. Facebook and others platforms enabled churches to provide online Sunday Services to their congregations. In this scenario, FB worked together for the good. Here was my opportunity to help someone by providing personal radiation details and reassurance. By using Messenger for our private dialogue, her courage increased through Christ to proceed with radiation treatments. I must admit, I am not as intimidated as I was previously to discuss the matter.

God healed my woundedness so that I might give an encouraging word to others. Then again, it would depend on the approach of the individual. I have learned that the Lord provides direction and peace when deciding who to help in their time of need. Individuals respond and receive differently from specific people, and that all depends on who God uses in their lives.

Do not feel discouraged when your voice is not heard or received by someone. It may mean that you are not the voice they need to hear from. Rejoice. You tried. Do not become offended or condemned. I could encourage her by sharing my experiences with radiation and how it was a completely unique experience than chemotherapy. After our dialogue through Messenger, she was at peace and proceeded with the suggested radiation treatment. She is doing well now. At the time of this writing, God brought me through a mastectomy, and prior to that a heart ablation procedure. Lastly, I had a simple mastectomy. I am now a '3,' a three-time survivor. Praise God, I am still here and want to give glory to my Lord and Savior Jesus Christ, my Heavenly Father, and the Holy Spirit for evening, morning, and noon. Always- '3.'

**The Louisiana Great Flood -August 2016**

"And my God will supply every need of yours according to his riches in glory in Christ Jesus" (Philippians 4:19, ESV).

God provided wisdom, strength and help from the sanctuary in the following three areas to walk through this trial:

1. Pre-planning through guidance of the Holy Spirit.
2. Favor to obtain an honest contractor.
3. Wisdom in using available funds to do more than I expected than home repairs and become debt free.

Barely three weeks after the final of four surgeries, a continuous rain fell in several southeast Louisiana parishes.

I live in East Baton Rouge Parish. Seventy trillion gallons of water landed over a period of less than seven days. This great rain dump has become known in Louisiana as the "Great Flood of 2016." Thousands of homes flooded that had never required flood insurance because they did not construct them in a flood zone. My home was one of those that did not require flood insurance, but God had it all planned out. Over 56,000 homes took on water and mine was one of them.

Perhaps now you can see all three life-changing events in less than 90 days (retirement May 26, surgery in June and flood August 16). The roaming from one experience to the next reminded me of the Hebrews in the wilderness. Which way next, Lord? Our walk of faith is not without trials and testing of our faith. I never had time to examine my current emotional and physical situations. God faithfully brought me through each event, although I really did not or could not recognize His faithfulness. I was on a day-by-day walk. That is why I share this testimony. Imagine if I would not have had health insurance at age 69 or health insurance that required expensive co-pays for each visit, especially specialists' visits. Imagine not having flood insurance? Imagine all this happening to a woman in her late sixties who is single, head of household, and retired from work for less than a month. I did not have to imagine this. God took care of me by gently leading me in what I would now call pre-planning in earlier years.

"And thine ears shall hear a voice behind thee saying, "This is the way, walk ye in it, whether ye turn to the right hand and when ye turn to the left" (Isaiah, 30:21 KJV).

Six years earlier in 2010, I received a letter offering flood insurance. I looked at it and felt impressed to pay the yearly premium, even though my home was not required to have flood insurance. God's pre-preparation for the "Great Flood of 2016" had unknowingly begun. I had an impression to buy flood insurance, although I never needed or was required to have it. I continued to pay a yearly premium for flood insurance for six years prior. Now, with a decreased monthly salary, I nearly dragged my feet on the 2016 renewal of the flood insurance policy. I thought to myself, *I do not live in a designated flood zone, and I do not have to buy flood insurance. I think I will not renew it this time.*

Yet, that still small voice impressed me to pay the premium "one more time." That voice I heard when I was hesitant to renew the premium in June 2016 said, "One more time." Why was I hesitant this time? I was in the natural increased to mode. Besides, the premium increased by $100. Thank God, the Holy Spirit helped me to be obedient, and I paid the premium in June 2016. Guess what happened two months later? That "Great Flood of 2016." I gave God all the praise and glory for speaking to me and His Holy Spirit helped me to hear and obey by renewing the policy. My insurance coverage included the contents and structure for my home.

This home has been my permanent residence for over 30 years and had never experienced flooding of any kind. God truly supplied all my needs for repairing and restoring my home. Those insurance premium payments paid off in 2016. God is good. I am thankful that I obeyed the promptings of the Holy Spirit. I was not homeless and I had a place to live. I hitched a ride with neighbors to evacuate and they brought me to my daughter's home. It was necessary because the waters rose swiftly. We had to evacuate immediately. My neighbor's oversized truck did the trick and got me safely to the part of town my where my daughter lived. There was no flooding in her area. I settled in for what would be seven months at my daughter's home. My daughter had her own living accommodations, and I thanked God for having a place to live.

I climbed three flights of stairs daily while living with her in her condominium. She lives in a vintage building which does not have an elevator. I climbed stairs while undergoing chemo and later radiation treatments. God gave me strength to drive myself to each of the 18 plus chemo treatments. I did not have to interrupt my daughter's work schedule.

My daughter is a compassionate young woman and she hung in there through all my surgeries. Even though she was my caretaker, I enjoyed waking up early and preparing her breakfast for her before she left for work each day. She was my best friend through recovery, chemotherapy, radiation, and repair of my flooded home. I went to treatments with my unseen companions, the Three in one, God the Father, God the son, and God the Holy Spirit. My designated holy angels encamped about me as well. Chemotherapy treatment and radiation schedules merged with daily visits to my home to check with my contractor and various necessary post-flood work. I had never experienced any kind of flooding in my life. I did not have a clue what was to come next or how to navigate through this newest trial that merged with the other two. I evacuated my home and left my SUV parked in a neighbor's driveway situated on a hill. I thought my SUV would not take on water there. It did. New adventures consisted of meeting my flood insurance agent and contractor, photos, going to and from the house, removing damaged furniture, appliances, and wet soggy clothes

God has good plans for us, and they manifested when He sent help from the sanctuary. Assistance for gutting my home came from the First United Methodist Church (FUMC). They gutted the entire house, and my home was ready for repair. A former neighbor treated my house for mold. Former students, coworkers, helped unload all the wet furniture, clothes, and other soggy items from our home. My son brought friends from out of state, and my daughter brought former college classmates form out of state as well.

A neighbor performed necessary moisture readings before re-construction of my home began. A former student who is phenomenally successful with his own business, brought his sons over with his electrician to inspect my home. So far, everything done for my home hasn't cost me a cent. God is faithful. Financial help also came from churches where I fellowshipped for many years, the Baton Rouge Symphony Chorus, Cancer Services, and two churches where I helped in the ministry. God made sure I lacked nothing. He is my shepherd, and I lacked nothing according to Isaiah 54).

My life was still terribly busy, and all the activities did not allow me to feel alone or lonely. I continued to sing with the FUMC Folk Choir and considered myself an affiliate member although I am not sure that even exists. I sang and rehearsed with the Baton Rouge Symphony Chorus in the Alto 1 section and served at three different churches. I did not have time to consider fear or self-pity, although my flesh longed to have a pity party sometimes. All of this happened while I still had the drain bag attached with schedules for chemotherapy and radiation placed on hold until the attending physicians removed the bag.

My Heavenly Father sent a helpful and friendly young man to serve as my flood insurance agent. I heard horror stories of people who had awful agents. Thank you, Father, for your provision of a compassionate young man to help me with my insurance claims and home. God provided every need.

A faithful sister in the church called me and asked, "Cheryl, do you need a contractor?"

I said "Yes!"

We made an appointment. I met him at my property and we made a deal for restoration. Hallelujah! God moved on my behalf.

Then the surprise came. After all these events, God allowed me to share my testimony worldwide through a brief video produced by the Christian Broadcasting Network's 700 Club. How miraculous could that be? They asked an unknown brown-skinned woman from

Winnsboro, Louisiana, whose home is now Baton Rouge, to share her testimony of God's faithfulness throughout the world. I supported the 700 Club for over 20 years and served as a volunteer with Operation Blessing years ago. Now, in my later years, I received an email requesting supporters to share their testimonies. I sloughed it off at first, thinking, this cannot happen to me. But God is amazing. After many phone interviews that took about three months and sending in verifiable legal documentations about events in my life, I was told they selected my testimony to be videoed and produced by CBN! The 700 Club sent a production crew to Baton Rouge to shoot and produce it. What a glorious Surprise to honor and give God praise for His love and faithfulness in my life!

I refer you to my testimonial video produced by the 700 Club and shown on the Christian Broadcasting Network. You can find the link below. As of this writing, I am still debt free by God's grace and mercy and owe no mortgage, car note, student loan or any other debt. The 700 Club video of my testimony can be accessed by to the following link:

700 ClubCBN (Christian Broadcasting Network) "Two Kids to Feed and No Salary" | CBN.com Link: https://www1.cbn.com/video/LEAD585v4/two-kids-to-feed-and-no-salary

"A man's steps are from the LORD; how then can man understand his way?" (Proverbs 20:24, BSB).

"Many are the plans in the mind of a man, but it is the purpose of the LORD that will stand" (Proverbs 19:22, (BSB).

"Come now, you who say, 'Today or tomorrow we will go into such and such a town and spend a year there and trade and make a profit'—yet you do not know what tomorrow will bring. Instead, you ought to say, 'If the Lord wills, we will live and do this or that'" James 4:13-15 (NKJV)

After seven months of house restorations, I could return to my home. God more than supplied all my needs, and I could budget in such a way that: I paid the contractor, purchased materials for restoration of my home, purchased new furnishings, my electric utility company DEMCO provided a furniture store gift certificate for new furnishings, my church provided a large cash gift check, the Baton Rouge Symphony provided a large gift check for chorus members, The miracle of it all is that I paid off the mortgage and car note! God allowed me to become debt free. That was the answer to my prayers from many years ago. All of this happened during the three trials of my life, all of them originating in a three-month period. It is Always 3.

# NOTES

# 3 – Lilith the First Wife

## Introduction

"All scripture *is* given by inspiration of God, and is profitable for doctrine, for reproof, for correction, for instruction in righteousness" (2 Timothy 3:16, KJV). Seeing names of women God used and how He used them in Biblical stories fascinated me. Isaiah, a major prophet mentions a female named Lilith in his proclamations. The Bible mentions her only once, but I wondered about her history. I began to dig, and I found out a few interesting facts from various sources.

"Lilith the First Wife," contains fictional scenarios, valid Scriptures from the Word of God that give meaning to fictional and non-fictional scenarios, and imagery. It addresses that great deceiver and fallen archangel Lucifer's plans to work through deception and blessings through allegiance to him. The reality is the opportunity for eternal separation from God. He is eternally doomed. Lucifer schemes continuously to deceive God's highest creation, His human children. Using his legions and eternal mate, Lilith, as a co-conspirator, Lucifer plots and schemes evil. God is described as the Great King. Lilith addresses Lucifer as the master and she discusses damning schemes to tempt and deceive humanity using evil suggestions. This first offering in the trilogy enlightens God's highest creation—humankind, about possible methods used by the adversary of our souls to steal, kill, and destroy!

"Thorns will grow up in its palaces, weeds, and brambles in its fortresses. It will be a dwelling for jackals, a home for ostriches. Wildcats will meet hyenas, the goat demon will call to his friends, and there Lilith will lurk and find her resting place. There the snake will nest and lay eggs and brood and hatch in its shadow. There too vultures will gather, each with its mate" (Isaiah 34:13-15 Common English Bible, CEB).

Lilith loved the sound of her own name and knew her worth to her master. The terrible and unclean lived near her fortress of weeds, brambles, and dark caves. Her origins as a demon spirit omitted by the writers of some European text and by those who excluded many ancient books of the Bible, did not inhibit her from her craftiness and workings for her master, Lucifer. After all, she knew many mortals knew of her existence. Since she is caught up in a timeless state, she further knew her existence was mentioned in the Torah, Talmud, and Midrash(1).

Her beauty and vanity allowed her to realize that she was a legend for her evil and cunning deeds. While continuing her dialogue with her loyal listening goat demon audience, she swooned, swayed spoke and thought about her eternal master/husband, her commander, Lucifer. She loved telling her story during the dark atmosphere of the evening's eternal stars and clouds and the sounds of hooves, winged demon creatures fluttering, and slithering snakes. Of course, her favored goat demon, Adulator, and his subordinates were present. She experienced power, glee, and self-promotion when sharing her damning joys with Adulator as he listened with awe, fear, intent, and total adoration. This was her temporary delight. Adulator prided himself on being the demon considered Lilith's best friend. He felt more important or higher than all the other goat demons. He always wondered how his Lilith, his lover, the first female demon, gained her status. He overheard some of the higher principalities discuss how Lilith chose to relinquish her dominion alongside of Adam as his first wife. He wondered what really happened.

Lilith continued to tell Adulator that she was created from the dust as Adam was by the Great King. She sometimes roamed the air, left her dark dwellings, looked about, and saw many of the principalities on their missions to their territories. The goat demon remembered how she constantly retold how she hated it when the Great King said to her there were limitations to her selections of fruit. She wanted to make her own decisions without apology, and she eventually did! This led to her downfall like that of her master, Lucifer. Her decision to yield to Lucifer and disobey the Great King caused her to be cast into everlasting abandonment and punishment alongside the one who subdued her. The Great King put Adam to sleep while He recreated the entire earth from the chaos caused by her disobedience, and that of her master, and his followers. They were left to roam the atmosphere and the deep abysses of the earth.

As she continued to reminisce, she retold the events to Adulator. She described what happened as Adam slept. Lucifer enticed her to come with him and indulge in tasting the sweetest of fruits. His beauty and giftings of music enamored her while she willingly went along with him. She completely forgot about Adam and was mesmerized by Lucifer as she began to eat and was intimately subdued by him and left her faithfulness to Adam and the Great King. She was the first female who entered the spiritual world of damnation who would lead rebellions of many mortals and participate in the reproduction of other demons as spoken of in Genesis 6,1-4:

> "When man began to multiply on the face of the land and daughters were born to them, the sons of God saw that the daughters of man were attractive. And they took as their wives any they chose. Then the Lord said, "My Spirit shall not abide in man forever, for he is flesh: his days shall be 120 years." The Nephilim were on the earth in those days, and afterward, when the sons of God came into the daughters of man, and they bore children to them. These were the mighty men who were of old, the men of renown" (Genesis 6:1-6, English Standard Version ESV).

Lilith continued to explain to Adulator that some of Lucifer's following of fallen angels reproduced living creatures with mortal females. Most of these creatures appeared to be fully human but had the partial powers of their master, Lucifer.

"Others reproduced by the fallen angelic beings with the daughters of men became giants, while others were like you, Adulator, handsome human/animal demons with powers from the master," she said. Adulator still wondered. Lilith continued, "That is why the Great King placed rules in His Great Book that humans were not to lay with animals as with humankind. My master and his fallen beings reproduced with both humankind and persuaded many humans to reproduce with animals as well."

Lilith told how she helped to entice the mortal females into rebellion against the Great King by giving mental and spiritual suggestions to them. She offered their minds fantasies of grandeur, physical pleasure, and power above their fellow earthly mortal females. Lilith continued the stories of how she also stole seeds form mortal men as they slept and reproduced demons who appeared human. Adulator wondered why many mortal humans did not know about this. She read his mind and became angry, which frightened Adulator. She told him that mortals only believed what they wanted to believe in the Great King's book and left the other ancient writings out of the it.

Adulator's subordinates trembled as she told the history. She continued to speak in her soft voice, as she remembered how her stay with Adam was good but not exciting. Lilith recalled how earth was incredibly beautiful, even before the Great King's Garden of Eden.

Once her master seduced her, the Great King threw the entire cosmos into chaos and put Adam into a deep sleep again. She gazed longingly at the vast realms of heavenlies as she remembered how the worlds looked before her disobedience to the Great King.

She remembered her own beauty she observed in the eyes of her master, the fallen angel of light in that first beautiful garden before the Great King threw everything into chaos. Lilith reflected on the glistening of the large dew drops from roses that were more than six feet tall and the size of a medium sized azalea bush. She felt she was much more beautiful than her successor, Eve. She even compared her own beauty and body to the women she would influence in the ages to come and believed herself to be superior. She had the same arrogance as her master! Her beauty, intelligence for cunning, and evil, along with her demonic powers assigned by her master, gave her extreme wickedness coupled with arrogance.

Along with the former Archangel Lucifer, she became the mother of night creatures. Her alliance with the Archangel increased her desire for wicked powers and she gained the abilities of evil influence upon humans. The Great King's creations by their own free will, opened their spiritual and mental doors to her. She informed Adulator that ancient writings gave her credit to giving birth to thousands of demons. She did so by collecting reproductive fluids from earthly males while they slept and brought them back to the evil spirit realms. She would not clarify to Adulator exactly how the process ensued, and he was too afraid to ask.

## Chapter II

Her specialty and assignment from the fallen Archangel consisted of mastering and leading all departed female souls who did not accept, obey, or know the Great King and to draw living souls away Him and His son. She continues to use her influence and powers to draw the quick or living humanity to reject the Great King and live lives of evil.

They would march on through mortality to become eternal tormented evil spirts. She would use them to influence multitudes before the end of the ages. Those she influenced had no idea what their deeds would lead to.

Many of those spirits she influenced were wicked women of renown who died in their wickedness such as Jezebel, Potiphar's wife, Delilah, Herodias, Lot's wife, and many more. Lilith influenced their lust, seductive dress, deceit, craftiness, and total rebellion against the Great King. She used her influence on any female who would give ear to her suggestions and not heed the voice of the Great King. Lilith's beauty became contorted as she expressed rage when she thought of female mortals she could not influence. An artic glaze of hatred consumed her eyes as she thought of names of those she could not consume. They included Mary the mother of the Great King's son, her cousin Elizabeth, Abigale, Esther, Ruth, and Rahab who repented and left her influences.

The Great King's words described Mary in his writings. She was obedient even when she did not understand:

"In the sixth month the angel Gabriel was sent from God to a city of Galilee named Nazareth, to a virgin betrothed to a man whose name was Joseph, of the house of David. And the virgin's name was Mary. And he came to her and said, "Greetings, O favored one, the Lord is with you!" But she was greatly troubled at the saying and tried to discern what sort of greeting this might be. And the angel said to her, "Do not be afraid, Mary, for you have found favor with God. And behold, you will conceive in your womb and bear a son, and you shall call his name Jesus. He will be great and will be called the Son of the Most High. And the Lord God will give to him the throne of his father David, and he will reign over the house of Jacob forever, and of his kingdom there will be no end."And Mary said to the angel, "How will this be, since I am a virgin?" And the angel answered her, "The Holy Spirit will come upon you, and the power of the Most High will overshadow you; therefore the child to be born will be called holy—the Son of God. And behold, your relative Elizabeth in her old age has also conceived a son, and this is the sixth month with her who was called barren. For nothing will be impossible with God." And Mary said, "Behold, I am the servant of the Lord; let it be to me according to your word. And the angel departed from her" (Luke 1:26, ESV).

Lilith knew the Great King loves obedience and there would be multitudes she would not be able to persuade. That would not stop her from attempting through various devious, orchestration, and persistent temptations to persuade millions throughout the ages into the snares for her master. Lilith knew from the proclamations and writings of the of the Great King's followers of old, that her master's destiny was eternal damnation.

She also observed from the portals of mortal time that some of the Great King's children continued to worship other mortals and material possessions. That made it easier to gain a larger following for her master. Many of them adored wealth and those who owned wealth. They wanted to be like them, even those who served the Great King desired to become like the wealthy prominent people who had sold their souls to her master. When that happened, the Great King would allow one of the master's lying spirits to entice obstinate mortals into further disobedience and damnation. That happened with as He did with King Ahab. In those instances, humans were allowed to choose and follow their evil passions. The Great King would give them space to repent but most of them did not.

> "And there came forth a spirit, and stood before the LORD, and said, I will persuade him. And the LORD said unto him, Wherewith? And he said, I will go forth, and I will be a lying spirit in the mouth of all his prophets. And he said, Thou shalt persuade him, and prevail also: go forth, and do so. Now therefore, behold, the LORD hath put a

> lying spirit in the mouth of all these thy prophets, and the LORD hath spoken evil concerning thee" (2 Chronicles 18:21-23, KJV).

Lilith explained to Adulator that many would not discuss her identity until millennials later. Most mortals would not recognize her because they did not read and accept some of the Great King's documents as valid. She knew history would identify many women of her influences. She laughed about it because she knew her deceptions worked and she loved that a vast number of females would worship her. After all most mortals believed Lucifer was the only one who enticed Eve.

In a way, Lucifer enticed Eve when he transformed his handsomeness and light into a serpent, but it was Lilith who approached Eve. Eve related to the female spirit and admired Lilith's beauty. Eve thought she finally had someone like herself to befriend…not knowing Lilith was an evil spirit. You see, Lilith appeared to Eve late in the evening when spirits roamed freely upon the earth before they returned to their realm. She saw Eve admiring herself in the pond and Lilith stood alongside her and greeted her. She startled Eve, but she was excited to meet another female.

Lilith was evil, perverted, and arrogant. She could have seduced Eve herself but her master craved to defile yet another of the Great King's females. He had already defiled Lilith; now it was Eve's turn to be deceived by the fallen being, the angel of light. Lilith never gave Eve her historical identity or the true story of being Adam's first wife. However, she told Eve of the beauty and delicious taste of the tree in the middle of the Garden. This left Eve with a desire to know more. Eve never thought to ask Lilith where she came from and wondered where she went when she vanished after the visit. Up to that time, Eve had never seen another woman. When Lucifer approached Eve as a serpent, the foundation was laid for Eve to disobey the Great King. It was not difficult to do. Eve no longer focused on the Great King nor Adam for she listened to who she thought was a female friend. That increased her curiosity about the delicious fruit. When the fallen supernatural being Lucifer approached Eve with his beauty, (even as a serpent) Eve was totally deceived and seduced.

Lilith said, "Some of the 'Great King's children disobey his son's words by continuously lording over others in arrogance and superiority. Many principalities' job was to take away their hopes by allowing others to think they are superior. Diminished success for the oppressed is wonderfully executed during mortal time by limiting their ability to function in current earthly time and society. A considerable number of the Great King's so-called children now worship political ideals and leaders, not the Great King. They have polarized his bride. This makes those afflicted, distracted from His promises and they now look to defend themselves. They have successfully been enticed to kill each other." Lilith smiled. "Such a wonderful thing. Pride, arrogance, an unteachable spirt and discord! The Great King hates discord! The assignment is to defeat all unity and love by instigating complete discord in the Great

King's remnant. Great achievements have been made in so called religious or Christian media in the 21st century. Those productions now offer political polarization programming and many of the Great King's followers no longer watch. What a joke! But it is success! Oh, but that remnant is difficult to defeat." She hated to say it, but they could not be defeated! "No one will ever defeat the Great King's remnant. They always hang around praying, worshipping, helping others, living holy and separate lives, and defending their faith in the Great King's Holy Spirit. It is difficult to get them to buy into worldly culture and come over to this side." Lilith squealed loudly with devilish laughter, still hoping to destroy and defeat the undefeatable remnant.

"When the ten heard about this, they were indignant with the two brothers. But Jesus called them aside and said, 'You know that the rulers of the Gentiles lord it over them, and their superiors exercise authority over them. It shall not be this way among you. Instead, whoever wants to become great among you must be your servant,'" Berean Study Bible (Matthew 20:24, BSB).

Lilith spoke again, "The Great King's words are known to all creation, even the trees and beast know the Great King's words and many stupid mortals believe and think they can get away with not honoring His Word! Good, they will spend eternity in the domain designated below for us and with us. They think and believe they are in control and label their control as belief in the Great

King." Lilith laughed so hard that Adulator trembled. "It has taken many earth years, but time means nothing to my master or me. We have deceived most of the Great King's flock and they do not even recognize they have been deceived."

Adulator asked, "Will we deceive them all?"

"Unfortunately, No," said Lilith. The Great King always has that uh, 'remnant' as well as His chosen ones from the original tribes. The lure and enticement can garner billions instead of trillions. The deceived will line up with the nations and go out to war against the Great King's son when He returns."

"How do you know this?' asked Adulator.

"It is in the 'Great King's text," said Lilith. "They continue to miss the mark while being caught up in outdoing each other and so-called 'walking in love' while overlooking the Great King's requirement for holiness. I hate holiness! But hey, we must get done what the master wants, we do not care how the Great King's flocks err. Not me! Many of the Great King's flocks have listened to our persuasion and have made idols of their churches, possessions, and even the color of their skin. Many of them dislike, hate, demean, are jealous of, and believe they are superior to each other for assorted reasons…so they walk in hate like us! They are deceived by thinking they are walking in unity but they are blind as some of the night creatures to the fact that they are not. Love has waxed cold or just 'left the building.' Many of them have been given over to reprobate or deranged minds and are not following the Great King's ordinances for male and female marriages and instead are marrying the same. They are now teaching their children to do so. Great victories have occurred. More than that of Sodom and Gomorrah."

Turning to Adulator she explained, "Oh, my dear Adulator, it is becoming a lot easier to deceive them, except for those few who still believe and attempt to live what the Great King's Word says. I hate, hate, hate them! They are hard to penetrate. Let us make sure we get as many of them as possible to abide with us in eternity. They still think they will abide with the Great King. I know we might not get them all but the master loves their worship. You see my dear Adulator, they worship the master when they willingly turn away from the Great King's Word. They love to imitate the world's culture in thought, actions, appearance, and philosophies. They follow the wealthy and popular worldly celebrities that we have promoted. Some are even given prominence in the Great King's sanctuaries, churches, and pulpits! The principalities do an excellent job. This is gloriously wonderful. Great progress is made."

Lilith squealed, "Eeee, we are doing such a wonderful job with those spiritual blinders! The master even said so. It is what the Great King said, 'in the last days many would fall away and be deceived.' Adulator, you must understand we know the Great King's Word but cannot abide by it. I find it strange that they do not believe their own Great King's words but rather believe each other and the ideas we implant in their heads. They dismiss many of His words because they reason, 'it's only mentioned once' in that Book. You know Adulator, they do what they call 'cherry picking.'"

Adulator wondered, *what is 'cherry picking'?* Lilith read his mind and told him, "That is when the mortals choose and manipulate a Scripture from the Great King's Word and twist it for their benefit. One example is when a doctrine, concept, or word in Scripture has no relevance or weight in their theology if only *mentioned once.*" Lilith squealed with delight. I wonder how they can say they believe what is in the Word of the Great King as His inspired of Word, yet they refuse to believe what He says. Still, they call themselves servants of the Great King. Their arrogance makes this much easier for me. Oh, this has made my assignment a lot easier. Ha, ha, ha, haaaa!" she laughed.

"Adulator, let me tell you, I came into being before Eve. You see, mortals do not want to recognize me because of their 'once mentioned' theory. That is fine. Many of the mortals and the Great King's chosen ones know the folklore and myths about me. Some believe them to be true but say nothing. Others dismiss me and have not the foggiest idea about my power of persuasion throughout the ages on their choices and temptations. As you can see my dear Adulator, my existence is true, and I delight to do my master's will, deceiving the mortals. Created from the dust like Adam, I was Adam's equal not helpmate. They will recognize me when they arrive in the same place with me in eternity…ha, ha, ha," she shrilled. Adulator wondered how he came about. Lilith answered his thoughts.

"Dear Adulator, you, and many like you came about before the time of a mortal named Noah. Others came during his time. The Great King's Word says this: 'Now it came about, when men began to multiply on the face of the land, and daughters were born to them, that the sons of God saw that the daughters of men were beautiful; and they took wives for themselves, whomever they chose. The Nephilim were on the earth in those days, and also afterward, when the sons of God came into the daughters of men, and they bore children to them. Those were the mighty men who were of old, men of renown, (Genesis 6:1, NASB).

Lilith continued to speak with Adulator and other listening fallen spirits. According to her, many of the master's followers from the Great King's throne began to have children with the Great King's mortal females. They also brought about perverted bestiality resulting in beings like yourself being born to mortal females. That is why you have the beautiful handsome head of a goat with beautiful human and angelic eyes and the rest of you look like a mortal man except for your hooves. Adulator did not know how strong and handsome he appeared even though his head was that of a strong handsome male goat.

"Adulator, you can seduce many mortals who do not belong to the Great King! You see, you appear as a demi-god. So, when the celestial portal opens for our activities, I will teach you what to do. Many humankinds in existence since the beginning of time, saw those like you and recognized their features in the heavenly diamonds in the night skies. The Great King had to make one of

His laws to prevent more creatures like you coming into existence," she stated.

"If a man lies carnally with an animal, he must be put to death. And you are also to kill the animal. If a woman approaches any animal to mate with it, you must kill both the woman and the animal. They must surely be put to death; their blood is upon them" (Leviticus 20:15, BSB).

Her explanation continued, "Adulator, this is how you were formed. Many of the master's fallen comrades mated with animals and comrades like you were created. That is why the Great King instituted the command against bestiality."

Adulator had several goat demons as friends who were his subordinates. He began to walk with a strange pride that he never had before. His eyes glistened in the dark and he had small wings on each of his shoulders. He had descended from humanity after being cursed while he existed on planet earth before he cooperated with the prince of demons.

She said, "There were many born like you and when the flood came, all like you perished and entered the realm with the master and me. After many rotations of the earth, the Great King then brought His completeness down in His majestic form and said He would replenish the earth. That is when He put Adam to sleep, eliminating his memories of me and created Eve from the dust using Adam's rib. Ha! When He created me, all my bones were mine. None came from Adam. The adopted race still does not understand 'replenish the earth' and what happened during that time." Adulator listened as she said, "The earth needed to be replenished after the Great King destroyed it after the master romanced me away from Adam. The Great King removed the giant creatures that roamed the earth, and the earth became void. The Great King and His completeness put Adam to sleep."

Adulator was surprised. He exclaimed, "I did not know all of that happened!"

"You could not have known Adulator; you were not in existence yet."

The Ram demon Adulator paced as Lilith told him about her eternal existence. Adulator had no recognition of earth time and did not know how long he had been in such a state. He only knew Lilith was unbelievably beautiful, and he was thankful he was her favorite.

Lilith flew without wings through the lower heavens, surveyed her latest assignment and reviewed the success of deceiving mortals. She said, "This did not take as long as I projected. Mortal time is ending, and we have much to do to deceive many more of the Great King's creations. We can continue to create disharmony, hatred, and now more demon worship. I do not know exactly when the end is, but I do know there are not many events left according to the Word of the Great King. We must increase our activities to gather as many as possible to our side of eternity. Only one thing hinders our assignments, torments, and destructions. They cannot be pursued without the Great King's permission that allows us to tempt them. They must choose to be a servant of the Great King or choose to follow evil suggestions. The Great King allowed the temptations and trials of His servants Job and Peter. Job survived and we almost had Peter, but he repented and turned away from us."

> "Now there was a day when the sons of God came to present themselves before the Lord, and Satan also came among them. The Lord said to Satan, "From where have you come?" Satan answered the Lord and said, "From going to and fro on the earth, and from walking up and down on it." And the Lord said to Satan, "Have you considered my servant Job, that there is none like him on the earth, a blameless and upright man, who fears God and turns away from evil?" Then Satan answered the Lord and said, "Does Job fear God for no reason? Have you not put a hedge around him and his house and all that he has on every side? You have blessed the work of his hands, and his possessions have increased in the land. [11] But stretch out your hand and touch all that he has, and he will curse you to your face." And the Lord said to Satan, "Behold, all that he has is in your hand. Only against him do not stretch out your hand." So, Satan went out from the presence of the Lord" (Job 1: 6, ESV).

"On the other hand, if the target is not faithful to the Great King's instructions, temptations can be pursued with great liberty. They do not even realize how soon their journey is over, yet they make plans and earthly policies that will change the destination of their descendants forever unless they use the unmentionable weapon." She referenced the God of Heaven's Armies and the power of His Word and the name of His Son, Jesus, but could not stand to say it out loud. She detested that name and her eternal mate hated it more.

Lilith continued to tell Adulator about her story and what her current assignment is now until the end of days. Adulator asked, "Did Eve ever know about you, Lilith?" "No, she said. Eve was clueless." Adulator still seemed not able to move forward with the story of Eve's fall. His curiosity grew even when explanations were given by his queen. "Wait, the master is coming," she said.

A great flow of light preceded her master for he is an angel of light. Adulator and all his demon friends trembled. You could only see red eyes peering from each of them as they perched in hiding. Lilith descended a little lower from her perched levels in the realm and waited to see her master. Her conversation was interrupted.

Lilith's master' asked, "What are you doing to insure we have more rebellion among those who say they love the Great King?"

Lilith responded, "I influenced many upper-level females who sing and preach, and those who are married to men who are pastors but wear provocative, revealing, and form-fitting clothing. They don't even realize the extent they distract their parishioners and cause them to lust during worship services. I also invaded traditional churches with the same sex-marriage doctrine by utilizing those who belong to us. They work in these churches to make it seem the Great King's words are irrelevant for their current culture and time. Another denomination continues to sexually abuse little boys."

"What did you use to influence them to go against the Great King and His Word?" asked a trembling Adulator.

Lilith looked at the fearful Adulator and said, "Pride, greed, and wanting more instead of wanting the Great King. Positions of influence, loving the limelight, and making others subservient to themselves at any cost of deception is also used through enticement. The Great King gave them over to a reprobate or degenerate mind. You see Adulator, we can make suggestions to their minds, and they think the suggestions originated from their own hearts. Sometimes their hearts are full of pride and longing for power. They do not realize when the influence comes from our realm." Adulator asked for an example of how that works. Lilith said, "There is always three things that can be used. The lust of the flesh, the lust of the eyes, and the pride of life. The Great King's' Word tells how it is done. According to 1 John 2:16, 'For all that is in the world, the lust of the flesh, the lust of the eyes, and the pride of life, is not of the Father, but is of the world.' Galatians 5:19 states, 'The acts of the flesh are obvious: sexual immorality, impurity and debauchery; idolatry and witchcraft; hatred, discord, jealousy, fits of rage, selfish ambition, dissensions, factions and envy; drunkenness, orgies, and the like.' Galatians 5:21 states, 'I warn you, as I did before, that those who live like this will not inherit the kingdom of God.'"

Lilith realized she had Adulator's full attention. She continued, "By using friends' influence and loyalty to the master, we facilitate whispers of discontentment. This affects their positions in life, spouse, popularity, home, or anything else we can use to increase their lust for more. We also make subtle suggestions through our connections with those who do not love the Great King but and famous in their secular visual and auditory entertainment. Even movies and music influence a portion of the religious churchgoers. They do not know the Great King and lust after popularity with the world. They desire to be like the world, and they hardly ever mention the Great King's Word because of …the pride of life. These influencers persuade the flocks to become discontent and they lust after other things as well. Strategic manipulation of the spiritually strong and weak cause them to be in the wrong place at the right time for the temptations to manifest and become easy to submit to."

Lilith knew enough is never enough. Rather than giving thanks to the Great King, His followers petition for more. Their desires are expanded by creating environments of discontentment and lust.

"You see Adulator, the set up never changes. It is always the same …the lust of the flesh, the lust of the eyes and the pride of life. Also, add the desire to mix the Great King's doctrines to deceive others and to make themselves popular like those who do not love the Great King. Our whispered suggestions work well along with setting up those who already serve us to appear to belong to the Great King. This makes them appear as loyal comrades of the Great King's flock. The seduction of fame and popularity has enticed some members of the 'flock to appear on secular shows. They are caught up in the fame, money, and pride of life they cannot verbalize the pure words of the Great King any longer. Why? They fear losing their fame and rejection from their worldly followers and supporters. Those supporters already belong to us. When they compromise the Great King's Word in their leadership position, it helps influence others who want to serve Him and lead them to eternal damnation. The flock has ignored and looked away from 'Keep your life free from love of money, and be content with what you have, for he has said, 'I will never leave you nor forsake you''' (Hebrews 13:5, ESV).

"What else are you doing to get as many of them as possible to worship me?" asked the master.

Lilith responded, "Many of the Great King's leaders are following what they believe to be love and mercy by allowing our worshippers to defile their sanctuaries. Many say they are called by the Great King to do His bidding, but they live in our realms of pleasure of known sins of adultery, fornication, and same-sex relations.

Large numbers are allowed to minister in the sanctuaries and are invited to invade pulpits to minister the Word, but they are hirelings. They only work for pay and a following. This seed of rebellion will produce much for us. 'If the high priest sins, bringing guilt upon the entire community, he must give a sin offering for the sin he has committed. He must present to the LORD a young bull with no defects''' (Leviticus 4:3).

Some of the Great King's flock ignore His Word. They do not apply much of it to their lives and many do not take advantage of grace and repentance though His son, Jesus, who is now the High Priest. Oh, I hate that name! We can still gain more worshippers because of the influence and deeds of those who follow us."

Her master smiled at her and began to caress her. Lilith then left that realm with the master for a season.

## Chapter III

When she returned, she continued her conversation with Adulator. Lilith expressed how much she abhorred that Holy Blood of Jesus which allowed mortals to be forgiven, establish right relationships with the Great King, and no longer be in bondage to the master. That all started when He decided to provide a way for the mortals to be redeemed from their grip. "The Great King sent one of His Archangels to that little maid named Mary that I mentioned earlier. I detest her! I could not get her attention! Neither could I gain the attention of others. Mary's son, the Great King's offspring came and changed our entire plan. He would offer a way of escape from eternal death with us. I hate speaking about it.

"The Archangel Gabriel would not join my master when he lifted himself up against the Great King. Gabriel, Michael, and myriads of other holy angelic beings stayed with Him and worshipped Him. There are more of them than us. The master told me about the event. He is still greater than those two if you ask me. Other female departed and living spirits have been aligned to deceive the Great King's offsprings and make sure their lust, pride, fame, and beauty keep them from serving the Him. The master created a rumor among those who serve him saying the Great King's son was not sin-free and that He adored one of the Marys. That lie is still floating down on the earth and fools believe it. They will serve the master's kingdom. They will not detect the tug of the Great King's

Holy Spirit any longer. Even when He sends His power through worship, they will be dull and backslidden and they will continue in the sins of their pride. That's exactly what the master did. After all, the master loved his own worship and rebelled against Him because he believed he was greater. I might not get all of them, but I will hinder them throughout their entire lives on the earthly domain until it will be too late to repent after they are dead. I will make sure they continue to be promoted in areas of influence, no matter how high or low. They will love their status so much that our realm will be adored and loved by them. They will depend on their new realm to exalt themselves with earthly influence and they will lead many others to our domain. I will entice them to defile the covenant of marriage. I will whisper to many females that their desire is no longer for one man but for men and women together. The Great King provided instructions concerning how they are to live, but they will ignore and overlook them and say the Great King's words are open for their own interpretations. Many others will say they have their rights and they can love who they want to and do away with human life. It is wonderful."

> "Then God said, 'Let Us make man in Our image, according to Our likeness; let them have dominion over the fish of the sea, over the birds of the air, and over the cattle, over all the earth and over every creeping thing that creeps on the earth.' So God created man in His own image; in the image of God He created him; male and female

> He created them. Then God blessed them, and God said to them, 'Be fruitful and multiply; fill the earth and subdue it; have dominion over the fish of the sea, over the birds of the air, and over every living thing that moves on the earth'" (Genesis 1: 26-27, KJV).

"The Great King declared the covenant relationship to be between one man and one woman in the beginning and reaffirmed it after we created the rebellion on earth when Noah was instructed to load pairs of male and females before the Great Flood."

> "Then the Lord said to Noah, 'Go into the ark, you and all your household, for I have seen that you are righteous before me in this generation. Take with you seven pairs of all clean animals, the male and his mate, and a pair of the animals that are not clean, the male and his mate, and seven pairs of the birds of the heavens also, male and female, to keep their offspring alive on the face of all the earth. For in seven days I will send rain on the earth forty days and forty nights, and every living thing that I have made I will blot out from the face of the ground.' And Noah did all that the Lord had commanded him..." (Genesis 7:1-5, ESV).

"Mortals cannot figure out the design for male and female from the Great King. It is recorded in His text that they who cannot discern their function have been given over to a reprobate or a deranged mind in Romans 1:27-29 and we will open doors for them to complete their derangements."

As she continued to speak, she was unaware of her master who listened while she told the story to the adoring demons. "Good," he said. Come with me for a while."

Lilith left with the master for a time with longing and great desire in her eyes. Adulator and his companions stayed behind.

When she returned, she said, "I must get more of the Great King's brothers and sisters of the lighter race to hate the dark race because of skin shade and their iniquity of arrogance. I will continue the lure of racial superiority and their need to dominate anyone who does not resemble their skin tone. You see Adulator, subliminal suggestions of racial superiority will continuously cause disunity in the Great King's Body. Many of that lighter skin race will instruct their children for generations to come, to live and dominate over others and snub the other creations as being inferior."

"How will you do this?" asked one of the demons. She continued her discussion.

"They love wealth, large houses, servants, territorial dominions, and self-elevations. However, they will not make fairness and access available to others not like them, difficult to achieve through their rule in government positions. Just watch. As the earthly years increase, they will pass this sin to many of their descendants who will become like them and our work is done. There will be generational hatred and arrogance! You see Adulator, there are always three, the lust of the flesh, the lust of the eyes and the pride of life. The Great King's Word describes how His Son was tempted by the master with the three, but He did not yield:

> 'And when the tempter came to him, he said, If thou be the Son of God, command that these stones be made bread. But he answered and said, It is written, Man shall not live by bread alone, but by every word that proceedeth out of the mouth of God. Then the devil taketh him up into the holy city, and setteth him on a pinnacle of the temple, And saith unto him, If thou be the Son of God, cast thyself down: for it is written, He shall give his angels charge concerning thee: and in their hands they shall bear thee up, lest at any time thou dash thy foot against a stone. Jesus said unto him, It is written again, Thou shalt not tempt the Lord thy God. Again, the devil taketh him up into an exceeding high mountain, and sheweth him all the kingdoms of the world, and the glory of them; And saith unto him, All these things will I give thee if thou wilt fall down and worship me. Then saith Jesus unto him, Get thee hence, Satan: for it is written, Thou shalt worship the Lord thy God, and him only shalt thou serve. Then the devil leaveth him, and behold, angels came and ministered unto him' (Matthew 4: 3-11, KJV)."

Adulator seemed a little perplexed, therefore, Lilith said, "Adulator, the same three areas are used to tempt the Great King's mortals. They love to lust for more and most would do anything for fame and a following. There seems to be a lack of contentment with many people, and this works well for the master. Some of the things they lust for appear to be good but many times, their motives are sinful pride, even when it is a good thing. " Adulator asked what should they do to entice the Great King's children using the three? Lilith said, "Observe their behavior when others succeed. If they are genuinely happy for them, it will be difficult to make them lust for more. Move in on the ones who pretend to be happy for others, to succeed. They will be an easy target to deceive into the lust of the flesh and the pride of life. Remember the story I told you about Ahab?"

She decided to give a recap. "Ahab was a king and possessed great wealth and we already enticed his wife Jezebel to the master's kingdom. Now Ahab worshipped foreign Gods instead of the Great King and wanted a piece of land that belonged to someone else. The owner would not let him have it, so one of the spirits lured and spoke to Jezebel. Jezebel had the owner killed and Ahab possessed the land without cost! Ahab lacked contentment so he lusted for the blessing the Great King had provided for someone else. Lust for mortals in the twenty-first century includes lust for increased power by using popularity, manipulation, oppression, and exclusion of those who get in their way. So, Adulator, divide your realms and armies into areas of deception making suggestions for lust of the flesh. Use any lie to create discontent in mental, emotional, physical, and spiritual areas. Make them believe the lie and injure others and themselves. Start with those large denomination churches, then move on to the non-denomination churches."

"Why?" asked Adulator.

Lilith said, "The master has successfully manipulated disappointment among the large following in the denominational churches, so we have considerable success there. Principalities have infected the base of each denomination. We see sexual abuse, wholesale adultery among the leadership, hideous racial, mental, and emotional abuse, acceptance of unholy unions of same-sex partners, and financial scandals. Their candle or lamp will be diminished except they repent. Magnificent work has been achieved by the principalities assigned to those denominations."

She continued, "Now, the disappointed followers of the Great King are moving on in hopes to find a better way to worship Him in a non-denominational setting. Let us wreak havoc in those churches as well. We already have many of their leaders addicted to drugs. Others have been unfaithful to their spouses, yet they continue to minister. Some have had their sex changed and pretend they were never what the Great King created them to be. We will manipulate them to disqualify His Word by reducing holiness to include and tolerate perversion, immorality, and murder with a demonic fake endorsement of love from their pulpits. They will say that the Great King's son is all about love and nothing else matters while we continue to steal, kill, and destroy. Parishioners will believe this great lie because it satisfies their pride and lust. They will believe anything to get their own way! Set up the whispers to their minds, arrange earthly time and dates for connecting them to the temptations, and make them feel their sin is not evil. Guide their rulers to make laws affirming evil, and then they will proceed to fall into our realms of eternal destruction. How wonderful!"

Still, she warned. "You must watch out for the mercies of the Great King. He allows His children time to repent. Revelation 21:2, states, 'And I gave her time to repent of her sexual immorality, and she did not repent.' Their sins will find them out. Then the schemes of the master will expose them to the world and destroy their testimonies and lives. You and many legions have excelled in bringing many of the Great King's children to the point of exposure. Very excellent deception!"

She continued, "One day, Adulator, the three from the master will go to war. The False Prophet, the Beast, and the Antichrist will war with the Great King's Son!" Adulator *wondered who are those three?* Lilith saw his thoughts and said she would explain at another time.

"The oppressed groups still cry out to the Great King!" Lilith continued discussing the plans. "I have seen how He answers their payers regarding our schemes. They will survive, but we will make it extremely difficult for them. A few of them will join the lighter race group and become traitors to their dark brothers and sisters. Our influence will be used by the lighter group to capture their darker brothers and sisters from other lands and bring them to a land they pillaged, murdered, and raped innocent females to acquire evil dominance. Once they raped the females, they then proclaimed themselves, holy, faultless, and became known as Founding Fathers. They preached and exalted others from the Great King's houses. In their desire for complete dominance, they will continue schemes throughout mortal time to disqualify equity, dismiss accomplishments of darker skinned people, and create systematic ways to make them fail."

She thought for a moment then sullenly stated, "Unfortunately, we will not be able to capture all the lighter group. Those we fail to reach will worship the Great King in spirit and truth and help their darker skinned brothers and sisters. Many of those lighter skinned will die for the freedoms of their darker skinned people. Mortals who listen and follow our prideful deceptions are entering the gates of hell and the lake of fire! They think they are doing a godly deed with their rebellion from one land to do what they call founding a new land, on the backs and blood of others. What they have done is plant a foundational seed of violence, hatred, and murder for the land they claim to have found. That seed will grow and make catastrophic fruit in due earthly season. They do not honor the Great King's Word which says they were all made from one Blood. They do not understand the Great King's Word about seedtime, and harvest or reaping and sowing. Violence, hatred, murder, greed will never leave their land because our duty is to make sure many of them continue in prideful dominant supremacy. This will yield explosive hatred as mortal time continues. Many, but not all the lighter descendants will continue to worship their ancestors by calling them Founding Fathers as if they are to be revered. They will neglect the humane needs of the people of their land for their own desires for titles, money, and material goods."

Her demeanor changed when she thought about their plan. "Oh, this will be amazingly easy. We have already planted the imaginations in their minds that they are superior. Keep pronouncing suggestions of inferiority to the darker skinned mortals and eventually a complete revolt will occur. Also, entice the darker skinned to self-inflict trouble by murdering their own. The lighter skinned ancestral inheritance of raping women, breeding children with them, and killing their own half-breed seed, while pretending to worship the Great King will increase but in a different form. What they planted will bring a future harvest of something they will call abortion. Many of the lighter skinned mortals do not understand or even attempt to acknowledge how the Great King created a relationship of Earth to the spirit world. The Great King created the earth with the ability to discern good and evil. An abundance of earthly time will pass before they feel the destruction from the innocent blood from the lands where they pillaged, kidnapped, and murdered. Here Adulator, let me show you a peek of what will happen. See, many darker shades of the Great King's brothers and sisters will be murdered at sea and their bodies claimed by the deep waters. Their lifeless souls and blood will cry out to the Great King from the depths of the blue deep. The Great King never overlooks the cries of innocent shed blood. Listen... hear what they are saying. 'Their ancestors submerged in the depths of the great seas will become sick and tired!' Many mortals think this is a myth. They will realize in eternity which myths are true and which are not."

"And the LORD said to Cain, "Where is your brother Abel?" "I do not know!" he answered. "Am I my brother's keeper?" "What have you done?" replied the LORD. "The voice of your brother's blood cries out to Me from the ground" (Genesis 4: 9, BSB).

"The weak mortal humans do not perceive the power of the Great King and His compassion on the weak neglected mortals. The Word about the Great King's son, Jesus Christ is the same yesterday and forever. Well Adulator, the Great King heard the innocent murdered blood crying from the ground. He also hears murdered slaves crying from the depths of the sea. It is quite easy to deceive those who have not pledged their allegiance to the Great King although they think they have. The Word declares that the earth responds emotionally."

"Trees of the field shall clap their hands" (Isaiah 55:12, ESV).

"Stones would cry out" (Luke 19:40).

"Tell the rock before their eyes to yield its water" (Numbers 20:8, ESV).

"So, Adulator, trees clap, stones yell, and rocks hear and obey! It is possible that the earth can respond to unnatural evils with regurgitation of energy through hurricanes along the pathway of the murdered dark innocent souls at sea. The whole earth groans (Romans 8:22-24) and 'reels to and fro like a drunkard,'" (Isaiah 24:20, NKJV).

As Lilith continued to explain things to Adulator, she turned up her lip in a wicked smirk of a smile and told how her plan was devised. She suddenly moaned with disgust and the demons' adorations ceased as they became fearful. They did not know what was wrong. Adulator wondered and she perceived his thoughts. She told how she could not move against some of the women because of the Great King's son, Jesus Christ. Jesus Christ was successful against all the temptations the master had attempted against Him. Now, the Son of the Great King had authority over all of them. Any one of His creations who believed on the Son would be saved from her master's eternal dominion if they continued to be loyal to the Great King.

Those receiving the Son as their Lord and Savior would be allowed to live forever in the eternal realm with Him and have no longer have fear, pain, nor influence any longer! She longed to commit to Him again, but she knew her loyalty to the master and her eternal damnation was settled as written in the Great King's Book. Even Adulator who was Lilith's favorite goat demon companion, wished, along with his subordinates, that they could have a different eternity. However, they were doomed forever to the bidding of Lilith and her master. Hate filled their hearts for the Great King, His Son, and His Holy Spirit.

Lilith continued to plan and discuss with Adulator. She sometimes used nonverbal communications. She projected thoughts into his consciousness as she told him that his job along with the legions he oversaw, is to always accomplish three things: inhibit the Great King's children by stealing their dreams and desires, kill their passions, and smear as many of their successes as possible. They were to destroy anything else related to their eternal loyalty to the Great King.

She said, "In mortal time of March 18, 2026, the assignment was to tempt those mortals who will give ear to change the western world's U. S. Constitution to allow a sitting President to run for a third term of office while tempting communist lands to destroy the western world through infiltration of their government. Humankind cannot discern how much we had to do with that. We are creating a dictatorship like our servant, Adolph. They cannot see clearly due to the log in their eyes. They have made an idol of their country! Oh, how glorious! They do not realize they left the worship of the Holy One, the Great King, a long time ago for the exaltation of their nation. They do not even know what that means. They no longer read the Great King's Word for worship and revelation. I hate to say anything about the Great King's Book, but we must know it to achieve destruction! Since now their nation is their God, everything is fair game when they yield to philosophies of their nation. Stupid mortals, all they need to do is examine the fateful havoc we wreaked on other historically famous lands to see how they fell and lost power!"

As she began to wrap up her history lesson, she shared more with Adulator. "Most of the population in the western territory is now enslaved like those who were under the rulership of our servant, Adolph. They are now sorry that they voted to extend the two terms for their leader. Their current leader has aligned himself with our advocate and he does not even know it. The bottomless pit and spirits from the lake of fire squeals with delight. How stupid could those mortals be? We now have the capability to enforce our next weapon. Oh, it is not a bomb. It is not biological and chemical warfare. It is intense and heightened mental, emotional, physical, and spiritual persuasion. Choosing the right variety is most important. Laws must be created to prohibit reading of the Great King's Word. We have influenced them, and they have yielded for so long that no one really recognizes our influences as evil any longer. They think that they are declaring their God-given rights."

All the goat demons wickedly laugh. Suddenly, their master comes to visit, and the laughter stopped.

"You are wasting eternal resources for the Lake of Fire. Get moving!" he said. "There are many more to influence. Complete the task assigned to you for those mega churches and finish up with the movie industry. Infiltrate them with wanton lust, adultery, idolatry, perversion, and the love of money. I expect this to be completed by my next visit. Remember, the task of three is to steal, kill, then destroy! I will watch the results of the commands I gave to the Prince of America."

The four bowed low and paid homage to their master as his light permeated their surroundings. In blind obedience and reverence, they did not dare rise until he left their presence.

******

School had just taken in at Park Place High in Baton Rouge, Texas. Abigail entered the classroom with her classmates, including her best friend, Jessica. They had been best friends since elementary school. "What are you doing tonight?" asked Jessica. "Are you going to mid-week service at church? Are you singing with the praise team tonight?"

Abigail was overly excited about going to church. Abigail said, "We have a new praise leader, and she wants us to dress more culture friendly, so we will not turn people off when they come to the church for the first time. Guess what? We were asked to get black leggings and wear a hip-length top and knee boots. I asked the new leader what about the Scripture that says, 'do nothing to cause your brother to stumble?' She asked me what I meant by that. I told her I was taught if I showed my figure or boobs it might entice my Christian brothers to lust. She laughed and said, 'They should know how to possess their vessel. You just wear what I tell you to wear.' "So, Jessica, I am excited about wearing what I like and not being concerned about my Christian brothers any longer."

"Somehow, that does not seem quite right to me, Abigail. Have you discussed this with your mom?"

"No, why should I?" Abigail continued. "She really does not need to know until after she sees what is going on, then she can say something. After all, our music is what we call 'cross-over'. Some people love our music because it appeals to those who really do not want to worship God but have their own way with other beliefs in God's house. You will understand later."

******

Lilith smiled as she and Adulator watched from their portal in the realms assigned for their habitations. The deep melodious voice of the spirit of Lilith laughed in the eternal realms. Her plans were succeeding. She reminded her underlings again how many mortal spiritual leaders rarely gave her notice since she is only mentioned once and only in the Old Testament Scripture.

Lilith hated rejection of her existence and being overlooked. It was an insult to only have a passing mention in the Great Book. She often spoke of that hatred. She worked diligently at conducting her master's orders. She is considered a power and a principality.

Adulator asked, "Why do I not see the dark-skinned humans in the western world any longer?"

Lilith explained and showed him mortal time. "Adulator, mortal time is not 2334. Do you remember when the chaos was created through their slavery, segregation, isolation, and dismissiveness through voting hindrances? Well, since the time of slavery, many of their leaders still held to underground beliefs and taught their descendants to acquire land in their mother land. Through the years, those who knew began the journey home, fed up with the western world treatment and now live peacefully in their ancestral home."

Adulator marveled at the current technologies of the dark-skinned humans and the joy they had. He said, "It appears they are loyal to the Great King."

Lilith said with great sadness and hatred, "Yes they are! Many of the Great King's offspring gaze at and are seduced by temporary mortal concerns and not the eternal promises of the Great King and His Son. Yet there are still those we cannot penetrate! You see, Adulator, we must do as much as possible because very soon, all things will end. We do not know exactly when, but the Great King's words tell of the end and our demise. The master is called Satan, the devil, Lucifer, and many other names in the Great King's Word."

Adulator listened while she quoted the passages from the Book. She finally realized hell was her eternal fate along with her master and his fallen angels.

> "I saw an Angel descending out of Heaven. He carried the key to the Abyss and a chain—a huge chain. He grabbed the Dragon, that old Snake—the very Devil, Satan himself!—chained him up for a thousand years, dumped him into the Abyss, slammed it shut and sealed it tight. No more trouble out of him, deceiving the nations—until the thousand years are up. After that he has to be let loose briefly. I saw thrones. Those put in charge of judgment sat on the thrones. I also saw the souls of those beheaded because of their witness to Jesus and the Word of God, who refused to worship either the Beast or his image, refused to take his

mark on forehead or hand—they lived and reigned with Christ for a thousand years! The rest of the dead did not live until the thousand years were up. This is the first resurrection—and those involved most blessed, most holy. No second death for them! They're priests of God and Christ; they'll reign with him a thousand years. When the thousand years are up, Satan will be let loose from his cell, and will launch again his old work of deceiving the nations, searching out victims in every nook and cranny of earth, even Gog and Magog! He'll talk them into going to war and will gather a huge army, millions strong. They'll stream across the earth, surround and lay siege to the camp of God's holy people, the Beloved City. They'll no sooner get there than fire will pour out of Heaven and burn them up. The Devil who deceived them will be hurled into Lake Fire and Brimstone, joining the Beast and False Prophet, the three in torment around the clock for ages without end" (Revelation 1:3, MSG).

## Judgment

"I saw a Great White Throne and the One Enthroned. Nothing could stand before or against the Presence, nothing in Heaven, nothing on earth. And then I saw all the dead, great and small, standing there—before the Throne! And books were opened. Then another book was opened: the

Book of Life. The dead were judged by what was written in the books, by the way they had lived. Sea released its dead, Death and Hell turned in their dead. Each man and woman was judged by the way he or she had lived. Then Death and Hell were hurled into Lake Fire. This is the second death—Lake Fire. Anyone whose name was not found inscribed in the Book of Life was hurled into Lake Fire" (Revelation 20:11-15, MSG).

## The Beginning of the End

"God so loved the world that He gave his only begotten son, that whoever believes on Him should not perish but have everlasting life. So, if you confess with your mouth and believe in your heart that Jesus is the son of God you will be saved. Do you believe? Then pray: "I believe in my heart that Jesus Christ is the son of God and I speak this aloud with my voice. Lord Jesus be my Lord for the rest of my life and show me how to live for you all the days of my life. Amen."

**God's use of the number three represents completion:**

Father, Son, and Holy Ghost (Trinity)

Lust of the Flesh, Eyes, and Pride of Life (Fallen Nature)

Christ Death, Burial and Resurrection (Redemption)

**Reference Page**


1. References:
2. Scripture References: Bible Hub- https://biblehub.com/context/matthew/27-14.htm
3. https://www1.cbn.com/video/LEAD585v4/two-kids-to-feed-and-no-salary
4. Common English Bible (CEB), Copyright © 2011 by Common English Bible
5. DROP: https://www.google.com/search?q=define+louisiana+drop+plan&rlz=1C1CHBF_enUS724US724&oq=define+louisiana+drop+plan&aqs=chrome..69i57j33l4.577321j1j8&sourceid=chrome&ie=UTF-8
6. Scripture quotations marked (ESV) are taken from the Holy Bible, English Standard Version, © 2001 by Crossway, a publishing ministry of Good News Publishers. Used by permission. All rights reserved
7. https://www.learnreligioms.com (Feb. 22, 2019)
8. Scripture quotations marked MSG are taken from THE MESSAGE, copyright © 1993, 2002, 2018, by Eugene H. Peterson. Used by permission of NavPress, represented by Tyndale House Publishers. All rights reserved.
9. Scripture quotations marked (NASB) are taken from Holy Bible: New American Standard Bible. 1995, 2020. LaHabra, CA: The Lockman Foundation.
10. Scripture quotations marked (NLT) are taken from Tyndale House Publishers. (2004). Holy Bible: New Living Translation. Wheaton, Ill. Tyndale House Publishers
11. https://www.biblegateway.com/

passage/?search=Revelation%2020&version=MSG

12. Scripture quotations marked (TLB) are taken from The Living Bible copyright © 1971. Used by permission of Tyndale House Publishers, Carol Steam, Illinois 60188. All rights reserved.
13. https://www.womeninthebible.net/women-bible-old-new-testament/naomi/

# NOTES

## About the Author

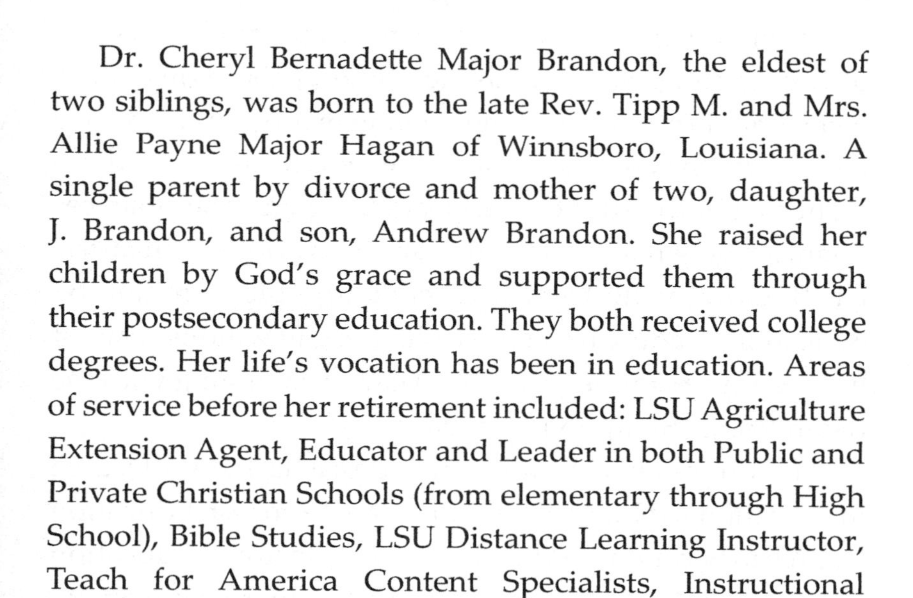

Dr. Cheryl Bernadette Major Brandon, the eldest of two siblings, was born to the late Rev. Tipp M. and Mrs. Allie Payne Major Hagan of Winnsboro, Louisiana. A single parent by divorce and mother of two, daughter, J. Brandon, and son, Andrew Brandon. She raised her children by God's grace and supported them through their postsecondary education. They both received college degrees. Her life's vocation has been in education. Areas of service before her retirement included: LSU Agriculture Extension Agent, Educator and Leader in both Public and Private Christian Schools (from elementary through High School), Bible Studies, LSU Distance Learning Instructor, Teach for America Content Specialists, Instructional Support Specialists, and Northwestern Louisiana State University Graduate School Adjunct Instructor.

Areas of Christian Ministry Leadership include Sponsor of Fellowship of Christian Athletes, Fellowship of Christian Students, Small Group Leader, Congregational Lay Minister, Praise and Worship Leader, Divorce Recovery Seminar Co-chair, Church Usher, Children's Church Leader/Teacher and wherever else God placed her. Dr. Brandon, a Spirit-filled believer by God's grace, earned her Doctorate in Special Education while working full-time (with one sabbatical leave) while putting her children through college. She helped with other events in their lives as they both served God and earned bachelor's and one earned a Masters' Degree as well. She is the grandmother of two high schoolers, Chandler, and Cameron and God mommy to one, Felton Jr. Her favorite method for vacation travel is Amtrak private accommodations. As of this writing, she spends her time encouraging other believers through speaking engagements, and various media platforms. She shares the goodness of God no matter what the situation appears to be and she practices financial generosity as God leads to various ministries. Dr. Brandon volunteers with philanthropic, community, educational, and Christian student organizations. One of her favorite enjoyments for five years was singing with the Baton Rouge Symphony Chorus.

Her professional training includes: a Bachelor's Degree in Vocational Home Economics, a Master of Education Degree in Secondary Education, and a Doctor of Education degree in Special Education from Southern University, Agriculture & Mechanical College. She received additional trainings and certifications from the University of Virginia as School Turnaround Specialists, Secondary Computer Science Engineering Instructor, Project Lead The Way (PLTW) at University of Texas Tyler. She holds Louisiana Department of Education Certifications in the following areas: Vocational Home Economics, Special Education, Parish or City School Supervisor of Instruction, Principal, Occupational Foods Service, Child Search Coordinator, Supervisor of Student Teaching, and Mild Moderate

1-12. God blessed her with these educational degrees and achievements, which allowed her to teach and follow her passion of educating youth and adults in both private and public sectors.

She published *Becoming Stronger in the Lord During and After Divorce,* Xulon Publishers 2012 and produced a musical CD entitled: *Amazing Medley*– Dr. Cheryl Brandon, Executive Producer; produced, mixed and mastered by Victor Smith, at Sanctified Sound, LLC.

You may email her at cheryljuly1@yahoo.com.

https://www.facebook.com/cherylmajor.brandon?mibextid=ZbWKwL

# NOTES

Made in the USA
Middletown, DE
08 September 2023

37724799R00106